Contents

Foreword

After the introduction of the National Curriculum for design and technology, it was immediately apparent that there was little published material relating to planning and implementing the subject in primary schools. The Design and Technology Association (DATA) planned a programme of publications which would provide support for both classroom teachers and co-ordinators. *The Guidance Materials for Key Stages 1 and 2* and *Planning into Practice* offer specific support for planning a broad and balanced curriculum and can be used alongside the National Scheme of Work; *Technical Vocabulary for Key Stages 1 and 2* identifies the key vocabulary which both children and teachers need to know and understand; *Primary Design and Technology – a guide for teacher assistants* provides useful information and strategies to help maximise the benefits of having an additional adult in a classroom and *The Design and Technology Handbook for Pre-school Providers* provides those who are involved in educating under fives with a comprehensive coverage of all aspects of design and technology for this age group. For the co-ordinator, *The Primary Co-ordinators' File, The National Framework for Supporting Design and Technology in Primary Schools* and *Volumes 1 and 2 of The Primary School Based Inset Manual for Design and Technology* offer support on all aspects of design and technology, including planned and resourced Inset sessions. Having provided a substantial range of publications which focus on design and technology to ensure that teachers gain a clear understanding of the subject, now is an appropriate time to examine the role of design and technology in relation to other subjects. *Research Paper 12: Cross-curricuar Links within the Primary Curriculum* sets the scene and provides a clear rationale for the links between design and technology and other subjects. This is being followed by publications which take a particular area of the curriculum and examine those links in more detail. It was decided that the first of these publications should be *Developing Language through Design and Technology* as all primary schools are focusing on language as part of the newly introduced Literacy Hour. It is anticipated that the book will provide much needed material to help co-ordinators, both of language and design and technology, and teachers as they examine their planning, identify specific objectives, and seek appropriate contexts for language work.

DATA would like to thank Professor Clare Benson for managing the project and, together with Julie Mantell, for writing significant parts of the book. The publication was made possible through the support of others. Glena Baptiste provided relevant information and resources focusing on language. Anne Jones and Jill Whittard have provided material for the Support section and offered comments on the final script. Kate Bennington, Angy Burn, Alison Hopwood, Helen Marron, Carol Martin, Gretel Roberts and Gillian Sheraton, have provided the useful case studies which indicate how theory translates into practice. DATA would also like to thank all those who provided useful comments during DATA seminars relating to the publication. The in-house editorial work was carried out by Natalia Link.

developing language through design and technology

DATA
THE DESIGN AND TECHNOLOGY ASSOCIATION

ESSO

First published in 1999 by DATA
The Design and Technology Association
16 Wellesbourne House
Walton Road
Wellesbourne
Warwickshire CV35 9JB

Section 1

The value of linking language and design and technology

1.1 Setting the context

Since the introduction of design and technology into the primary curriculum, the notion has been promoted that language can be developed through design and technology. However, it is not sufficient just to say that; action has to be taken to identify the 'why, what, how and when' to ensure that appropriate links are made and that this is achieved in a structured and organised way. Of course, there will always be unexpected opportunities and the value of these should not be dismissed. But if children are to develop all aspects of their language skills, this cannot be left to chance.

With the government's focus on literacy and numeracy, now seems an appropriate time to explore the relationship between design and technology and these areas of the curriculum in depth as it is important when any links are made that they are integral to teaching and learning. The intention in producing this book is to show why and how links should, and can, be made. It is anticipated that other books in the series will focus on links with mathematics, science, ICT and art.

1.2 Why 'language' not 'literacy'?

As a practical subject, which involves children in both thinking and doing, design and technology provides many opportunities for children to develop speaking, listening, reading and writing skills. As this book sets out to identify purposeful links between all aspects of language and design and technology, it is important that all aspects of the subjects are covered in the title. Teachers have to deal with several documents when planning. The Literacy strategy 'unites the important skills of reading and writing. It also involves speaking and listening ... which are not separately identified in this framework'. Whilst it is expected that teachers should include Speaking and Listening in the Literacy Hour, explicit objectives are not included in the framework and teachers

have to refer back to the National Curriculum documentation for the content that has to be covered. Teachers know that many aspects of language are included in the programmes of study for the National Curriculum for English but there is still additional content in the Literacy framework that needs to be taught. By using the word 'language', it is the intention that the readers will understand that all aspects are examined and given appropriate importance in differing situations, thus enabling purposeful links between the two areas to be made.

1.3 Language for learning

Children's use of language is a vital skill that influences their progress in every area of the curriculum. Through a wide variety of activities in school, children have the opportunity to learn to use language, to use language to learn and to learn about language (Bearne 1998). Language is a tool for thinking and communication and design and technology can offer an exciting context for children to become more skillful in using this tool. Eve Bearne's (1998) useful summary showing how language fits into learning mirrors much of the designing process and it is up to the teacher to ensure that children have the opportunity to use an appropriate range of language to take their learning forward.

Children use language for:
- Preparation, getting ideas going, framing questions.
- Gathering, organising or categorising information.
- Exploring ideas, hypothesising, predicting, describing, persuading, arguing.
- Giving information to others, communicating ideas.
- Reflecting on and evaluating learning, reviewing progress.
- Demonstrating that something has been learned.

1.4 Using different aspects of language

As teachers, we all understand the importance of giving children opportunities to develop as effective users of spoken and written language. This philosophy underpins the programmes of study for English and is also significant in other curriculum areas. However, design and technology and language have a particularly symbiotic relationship which we can exploit in order to enhance the teaching and learning in both subject areas.

Many of the skills we need to teach, particularly in design and technology, depend on developing children's ability to communicate effectively. In Key Stage 1 the English programmes of study for Speaking and Listening require children to have opportunities to describe experiences and explore, develop and clarify ideas. In design and technology, to develop designing skills, children should be taught to draw on their experience to help generate ideas, and to clarify their ideas through discussion. Further comparisons reveal the need to encourage predicting outcomes and discussing possibilities, and make suggestions about how to proceed. The point is that in encouraging children to articulate their ideas, recount their experiences or give reasons for their opinions or actions, we are teaching transferable skills. Some children will find that design and technology activities give these experiences a tangible context which they find easier (or simply more interesting) to articulate.

At first the focus tends to be on spoken communication, but by producing a design in the form of a drawing, children can record their design ideas. Labelled drawings give children a real reason for writing, and lists of the equipment or materials required for the making process are useful to introduce the appropriate vocabulary and to contribute to the range of writing which the children experience. They can then begin to record their understanding of the process of development in increasingly sophisticated ways. Some schools use writing frames, such as those developed by Wray and Medwell (1995), to support the children until they are familiar with a particular genre.

The need to read, both their own texts and a variety of other sources, will ensure that children engage with information texts. These may include ICT based reference materials or, at Key Stage 2 relevant material not specifically produced for children. It is well documented that children often need more support in tackling unfamiliar information texts (Neate 1993). Modelling how we read these differently from fiction is important and shared reading of such texts is useful if the children are going to produce their own factual account, for example, when evaluating a product.

In both language and design and technology, at Key Stage 2, children are expected to develop a greater awareness of the purposes and audience/users for their work and we should highlight this overlap. We should aim for a balance of independent and collaborative work which encourages children to synthesise their skill, knowledge and understanding and enables them to communicate effectively.

1.5 The benefits of linking language and design and technology

Through linking the two subjects, the advantages for both children and teachers are readily apparent.

For the children, the benefits include:
▌ **a real need**
design and technology activities offer children a real purpose for using and developing their language skills
▌ **relevant contexts**
design and technology provides the variety of relevant contexts which children need to be able to use and develop their language skills
▌ **the opportunity to apply language**
there are opportunities to apply all types of language and to gain practise in areas in

which a child finds a particular difficulty. For those who have English as a second langauge, design and technology is a useful vehicle through which language development can take place in meaningful contexts for the children.

▌enjoyment

there is a growing body of evidence which suggests that children reach higher levels in language, particularly in writing and speaking, through design and technology as they are so well motivated (see Case Study 1).

For the teachers the benefits include:

▌planning within meaningful contexts

when planning for the Literacy Hour, it is useful to find meaningful links and contexts for the children to aid learning

▌assessment opportunities

as language opportunities within design and technology are varied and purposeful, there are many situations when teachers can assess children's use and application of language. Children may well perform better in certain contexts

▌best use of time

with the constant pressures that are placed on the primary timetable, it is crucial that work is not unnecessarily duplicated. Careful planning is needed to ensure best use of time.

Section 2

Opportunities for developing aspects of language in design and technology

2.1   Introduction

This section describes the types of speaking, listening, reading and writing which form a natural part of children's learning in design and technology. The three types of activity in design and technology: investigative, disassembly and evaluative activities (IDEAs), focused practical tasks (FPTs) and designing and making assignments (DMAs), require children to use language in a variety of ways for real purposes. This helps to make design and technology a valuable context in which children can apply and develop their learning from more structured language sessions. Section 3 describes different approaches to planning that might support teachers in making the most of the links between language and design and technology.

2.2   Speaking and listening in design and technology

Most design and technology activities involve children speaking and listening in informal or more structured ways. Children use speech as a way of expressing themselves, exploring their thinking, reflecting and communicating with others.

Children might be speaking and listening to a variety of different people as part of their work, i.e. each other, the teacher, teacher assistants, visiting experts or possible users of their products. This will require children to communicate in different ways using appropriate methods of expressing themselves and accurate vocabulary. For example, the style of language used in a class brainstorm will be different from asking questions in a survey or from presenting their work in a class assembly.

Children need to have the opportunity for both exploratory and presentational talk. Exploratory talk might be involved when they are evaluating a product, suggesting ideas, planning with other children, negotiating with a partner or even talking aloud to themselves, as many of us do when attempting to solve a tricky problem. Thinking aloud is a vital part of our thought process, as we try to sort ideas and make decisions. For some children this process will be aloud, for others it will be silent as their inner voices do the talking inside their heads. But whether silent or aloud it is important to recognise the value of language as a tool for thinking as well as for communicating. Presentational talk involves children in having to plan and this process of preparing and rehearsing can help to clarify thinking as well as requiring them to communicate effectively to a particular audience.

We can help children to develop their thinking in design and technology by giving them opportunities to talk and to listen to others in different situations and for different purposes (see example on page 11).

Encouraging quality speaking and listening in design and technology

Although speaking and listening will naturally take place during activities in design and technology we can support children in improving the quality of their talk and listening in a number of ways. This will involve making sure that all children have a wide range of opportunities for different types of talk and listening, supporting them in learning technical vocabulary and encouraging them to use language appropriately and effectively in different situations.

Consider the following strategies for encouraging quality speaking and listening. To what extent do you already use these strategies when planning or working with the children? What other strategies do you find helpful?

Strategies for encouraging quality speaking and listening in design and technology

■ provide opportunities for children to talk to different audiences, e.g. to a partner, to other children in a group, to the whole

Design and technology situation	Speaking and listening
A class discussion at the beginning of a project.	Responding to a stimulus, sharing past experiences, suggesting and listening to ideas.
Designing with a partner.	Exploring, developing and clarifying ideas, planning and reflecting.
A group brainstorm.	Generating ideas, listening to others.
A demonstration of a technique.	Listening carefully, remembering and responding, following instructions.
Investigating a collection of products.	Describing, naming, comparing, sorting, identifying similarities and differences, developing vocabulary.
Disassembling a product.	Explaining how something works, naming component parts and materials.
Finding out about people's preferences.	Asking questions, explaining, listening.
Finding out from non-fiction texts.	Posing questions, reporting back to others.
Discussing design ideas.	Suggesting, speculating, listening to feedback.
Reporting on their work.	Explaining, describing, presenting.
Planning their making.	Planning, predicting, negotiating.
Asking for help.	Asking questions, listening and responding.
Making judgements about their final product.	Reflecting, analysing, evaluating against criteria.
Evaluating while they are making.	Reflecting, commenting, suggesting.

class, to the teacher, to other adult helpers, to older or younger children, to visitors, to the whole school
▌ help children to become aware of how they need to consider their audience, e.g. speaking clearly to a larger group, speaking with expression, listening to what others say, learning when it is appropriate to interject and when it is not
▌ structure discussion activities so that there is a clear sense of purpose and all children are actively involved, e.g. a whole class brainstorm where each child is encouraged to contribute, using circle time to discuss a particular product – what it does, how it works, how it is made, who might use it etc.
▌ use different group work techniques, such as the jigsaw method, to focus group discussions and give a clear purpose to children's talk
▌ introduce new technical vocabulary and encourage its use
▌ provide opportunities for children to talk for different purposes, e.g. explaining how something works, giving instructions,

exploring ideas, clarifying ideas and making plans, reflecting on their work, presenting to other people, asking questions
▌ value children's talk and its role in learning, e.g. talking about purposes of talk with children, sharing examples of when it has helped to talk through an idea or problem
▌ support other adult helpers working in the classroom by discussing the types of questions and talk that encourage children to discuss their work
▌ give time for children to answer questions
▌ listen to children when they talk to you and each other
▌ use questions that encourage children to think, to speculate and to express their views and thoughts, e.g. What would happen if...? What do you think about...?
▌ use talk other than questions to stimulate more two way discussion, e.g. making suggestions, responding to their work, expressing your own thoughts and views
▌ do not assume that children are listening just because they are looking at the speaker/s; conversely do not assume that

they are not listening because they are not focused on the speaker/s
∎ provide opportunities for children to show how well they have listened and understood. They could write notes as they listen and feed back their key points to others; tell others three important points that they have identified from a talk; write a report on something that they have listened to; create an information sheet which could include drawings, labels and notes; make a model using e.g. construction kits following verbal instructions.

The work of the National Oracy Project provides more detailed information about improving children's speaking and listening including case studies and examples of teaching strategies. Details about publications from the project are given in Section 6.

2.3   Reading in design and technology

The National Curriculum for English and the National Literacy Strategy provide detailed guidelines on aspects of reading to be covered at different stages. Much of this work will take place in specifically focused literacy sessions. However, design and technology, along with other subjects, will provide children with a context for developing their skills in reading. In design and technology children will be involved in reading at word, sentence and text levels and will need to use a range of non-fiction and fiction texts to help them in their work.

Purposes for reading in design and technology

Children will need to read for a variety of purposes as part of their design and technology activities, including:
∎ finding out about techniques, e.g. using non-fiction texts to find out about flour and water batik or different types of switches
∎ finding out the meanings of technical terms
∎ finding out about how things work
∎ finding out about users' views, e.g. reading the results of a questionnaire or survey

∎ following instructions
∎ as a stimulus for ideas, e.g. reading traditional stories to get ideas for puppet characters, looking through recipe books
∎ for reminding, e.g. a checklist of things to do, a list of tools and materials needed, a step by step plan, a list of criteria for a product
∎ as models for different types of text, e.g. recount, explanatory, instructional, discursive, persuasive.

Types of texts used in design and technology

To support a greater emphasis on reading, teachers and co-ordinators will need to make available a wide range of appropriate texts. Texts may be in a variety of forms such as books, posters, charts, worksheets, instruction cards, captions on displays, labels, leaflets, CD-ROM and websites. In design and technology useful texts might include:
∎ texts that help children to do, e.g. recipes, safety rules, instructions
∎ texts that help children to find out, e.g. dictionaries, glossaries, word banks, encyclopedias, non-fiction books, posters, websites, CD-ROM, reference books
∎ texts for stimulating ideas, e.g. recipe books, shopping catalogues, craft books, stories, poems, plays, examples of particular types of text
∎ texts for analysis, e.g. instructions, advertisements, official documents related to design and technology, non-chronological reports, newspaper articles
∎ children's texts, e.g. notes, lists, ideas, a designing diary, design criteria, captions for display, class books, instructions, letters, questionnaires, brainstorms, annotated drawings
∎ teachers' texts, e.g. notes, pro formas for guiding thinking, writing frames, instructions, captions for display, labels, lists, planning flowchart, particular types of texts modelled for children, design sheets.

Encouraging quality reading in design and technology

There are many opportunities for reading for real purposes in design and technology.

Some reading will be at a level that stretches children whereas some should be manageable for children to read independently. Children will need help in extending their sight vocabulary, understanding technical terms, reading whole texts for understanding and accessing relevant information from a range of texts. There may also be occasions when children need help in learning to read expressively to present their work to others.

Consider the following strategies for encouraging quality reading. To what extent do you already use these strategies when planning or working with the children? What other strategies do you find helpful?

Strategies for encouraging quality reading in design and technology

∎ providing a range of suitable texts, e.g. at an appropriate reading level, accessible, attractive presentation, relevant information, different forms and text types
∎ planning opportunities for children to read for real purposes, e.g. instructions, playscripts to go with their puppets, their own notes, pro formas to guide thinking, flowcharts to help in planning
∎ encouraging children to enjoy reading and finding out, e.g. having attractive books and other reading resources, sharing favourite examples with children, giving children time to browse, making class books available for children to enjoy
∎ introducing technical vocabulary and encouraging children to use it, e.g. by using captions on displays, word banks, dictionaries, glossaries, labelling tools and materials
∎ helping children to develop their skills in using texts, e.g. increasing their sight vocabulary, giving them opportunities to practise using indexes and lists of contents, showing them searching techniques when using the Internet, teaching them techniques to help them to access information effectively, helping them to

develop their understanding of what they are reading by relating it to what they already know
∎ planning focused activities using texts, e.g. using a KWL grid when using non-fiction texts (What do you know? What do you want to find out? What have you learnt?), reconstructing a text in a different form such as an annotated diagram, finding the meanings of technical terms using reference books
∎ supporting children with reading difficulties, e.g. selecting appropriate texts, presenting text in an alternative form that is easier for children to access, paired reading, helping children to recognise key vocabulary before reading the whole text.

When children are working in design and technology they will need to write for a variety of audiences such as themselves, other children, their teacher, parents and members of the local community. Writing in design and technology is usually a product of speaking, listening and reading. It will appear in a variety of forms and children will need to learn about different styles of writing used for different purposes and occasions. Writing that records their thinking or helps to organise ideas will often need to be quick and exploratory, whereas writing used as a way of communicating with others in a more formal way will need to be carefully thought through so that the language used is accurate and well presented.

The National Curriculum for English and the National Literacy Framework provide detailed guidance on aspects of writing to be covered at different stages. As with reading, many of the specified objectives will be planned into literacy sessions. However, design and technology, along with other subjects, provides an opportunity for children to apply their knowledge and skills in a real context.

Purposes for writing in design and technology

There are opportunities for children to write at word, sentence and text levels for a variety of purposes in design and technology:

∎ to help their thinking, e.g. plans, annotated drawings for their designs, flowcharts, a group brainstorm, possible solutions to a problem

∎ to act as a reminder, e.g. lists of things to do or materials needed, a list of criteria for their design, safety rules, notes taken after the demonstration of a technique

∎ as a way of reflecting, e.g. keeping a designing diary, writing comments against their list of criteria to say how well their product has met each of the criteria, writing an evaluation of their work

∎ as a way of recording, e.g. adding comments to their original design to show changes made and why, writing about what they did, recording the results of an investigation that will inform their designing and making, using a pro forma to record the stages of their work

∎ as a way of communicating, e.g. writing a letter thanking a visitor who has helped them with their design and technology, writing a message to another member of the group, making a caption for a display of work, writing about their design ideas

∎ as a way of finding out, e.g. writing a letter requesting information, writing a questionnaire, making notes from a non-fiction text, writing a list of questions before using a non-fiction text, filling in a chart that focuses their attention on different aspects of the products they are investigating

∎ as part of their outcome, e.g. practising lettering for their message in a greetings card, writing appropriate text for the outside of their packaging, writing an advertisement to promote their product, making a moving storybook for younger children

∎ as evidence of their learning, e.g. answering written questions, writing an explanation of how something works, writing a set of instructions to show they know how

to do something, writing definitions of technical terms.

Types of writing in design and technology

Children need to be given the opportunity to write for different purposes and audiences and to apply what they learn about different genres.

Examples of writing in design and technology include:

∎ writing for themselves: notes, annotated sketches, lists, glossaries, designing log, criteria, flowcharts, plans, storyboards

∎ writing for others: signs, labels, captions, recounts, messages, letters, reports, instructions, explanations, plays, stories, newspaper articles, leaflets, posters, advertisements.

Encouraging quality writing in design and technology

There are many opportunities for using different types of writing in design and technology activities. Children will need help to recognise the purposes of writing and how to write appropriately for different audiences. In design and technology children will use writing to express and communicate their ideas alongside speaking, working with materials and drawing. We need to encourage children to use the most appropriate form of communication, for example, an annotated drawing to show their design ideas or a storyboard with drawings and words to show how they made a model. Children also need to consider their handwriting, for example, when to use a clear, neat hand for presented work and when a quicker hand can be used for note taking and drafting. The computer may be used for drafting and editing work, group writing or for presenting a text using appropriate layouts, fonts and point sizes.

Producing a finished piece of writing for an audience other than oneself is a similar process to designing and making a product in design and technology and it may be helpful to draw older children's attention to these similar processes.

developing language through design and technology

Writing	Designing and making
Considering the needs of an audience.	Considering the needs of the user.
Generating ideas through discussing, brainstorming and other techniques.	Generating ideas through discussing, brainstorming and other techniques.
Planning using a flowchart, a storyboard or other techniques.	Planning using a flowchart, a storyboard or other techniques.
Editing and redrafting.	Modelling
	Evaluating and modifying.
Reading texts as a stimulus for ideas .	Investigating products as a stimulus for ideas.
Analysing texts to learn about features of particular types of text.	Analysing products to learn about features of particular types of product.
Investigating words and language structures.	Investigating materials and ways of making.

Teachers can support children's writing in design and technology in a variety of ways. Consider the following strategies. To what extent do you already use these strategies when planning or working with the children? What other strategies do you fnd helpful?

Strategies for encouraging quality writing in design and technology

▮ planning opportunities for children to write for real purposes and audiences, e.g. making lists to remind themselves, writing an invitation to other children to a picnic, writing captions for a class display, writing instructions for a partner to follow, writing a list of criteria for their product
▮ planning writing activities that build on children's speaking, listening and reading, e.g. recording ideas from a group brainstorm, reconstructing a text in a different form, making a group proposal for their design, writing a catalogue to describe a group of products that the children have been investigating in groups
▮ planning opportunities for children to write different types of texts, e.g. explaining how a mechanism works, a recount describing how they made their product, a recipe, a story brought to life with moving parts for younger children
▮ recognising the possibilities for children combining writing with other forms of expression, e.g. annotated drawings,

illustrated sets of instructions, recording notes from a group discussion, writing captions to accompany examples of making techniques, making an illustrated poster of safety rules
▮ modelling language for children, e.g. creating a set of instructions together, drawing children's attention to the features of instructional texts
▮ providing good and poor examples of writing and discussing the differences, e.g. evaluating instructions
▮ providing scaffolding and other forms of support for children's writing, e.g. writing frames, charts for children to fill in with information about products, displaying key words, providing examples of different types of texts
▮ encouraging children to use technical vocabulary accurately, e.g. displaying key vocabulary for a unit of work, providing dictionaries and glossaries, encouraging children to make on-going glossaries of technical terms
▮ providing children with opportunities to publish, e.g. individual, group and class books, posters, writing articles for school magazine or website
▮ talk about common processes between writing and designing and making a product, e.g. thinking about the needs of users/audiences, similar techniques for designing and planning, evaluating and modifying/editing and redrafting.

Section 3

Planning strategies

3.1 Introduction

To make any links effective, planning is the key to success. In the past there have been few attempts to really structure the links between language and design and technology and to highlight the activities which provide the most appropriate and useful opportunities to introduce and extend language. As all schools have access to a scheme of work for design and technology, either their own or the national scheme of work, now is the time to put the planning into place. There are a variety of ways of tackling the planning but communication between co-ordinators, and between co-ordinators and the rest of the staff is vital if the development of the links is to be successful.

The language focus can be highlighted in the plans for design and technology, for language or for both subjects. It may be appropriate for aspects of language to be covered in the Literacy Hour where the opportunities relate to a design and technology context.

> **Example**
> **Literacy objective:** Text level work; Non-fiction writing composition – to write simple questions.
> **Year 1 Term 2**
> In the Literacy Hour, the children write questions as they begin to evaluate a product e.g. what is it made of? who uses it?

However, it may be more appropriate for the language to take place in a design and technology session and the appropriate language objectives would be included in the design and technology planning.

> **Example**
> **Literacy objective:** Text level work; Non-fiction writing composition – making notes.

> **Year 4 Storybooks**
> DMA – making notes to help in planning jobs to be done, allocating tasks and keeping a record of what has been achieved.

Where such real opportunities exist, the teacher can model the writing in design and technology or remind the children of activities carried out in the Literacy Hour.

There are two aspects of planning which are covered in this section. The first relates to planning links in the whole school context; the second relates to planning links across the curriculum.

3.2 Planning links in the whole school context

The development of effective links between language and design and technology will be the concern of both co-ordinators and individual class teachers and the following strategies provide a range of ideas to trial.

Strategies for the design and technology co-ordinator

▌ become familiar with a range of opportunities for developing language in design and technology
▌ be prepared to show others, e.g. governors, parents, class teachers, how design and technology can provide a motivating context for developing language, e.g. by running a workshop, writing a leaflet, making an input at a meeting
▌ provide an input into any meeting in school relating to literacy and language development to show how it needs a context and give examples from design and technology
▌ include a section in the school policy on how language can be developed through design and technology
▌ plan the links with the language co-ordinator on a whole school plan
▌ encourage teachers to include examples of language developed within design and

technology on displays and in class assemblies
▌ become familiar with a range of fiction and non-fiction texts related to design and technology and share examples with the language co-ordinator and class teachers
▌ share successful examples of teachers' planning and children's work in language linked to design and technology
▌ include relevant examples of children's language in design and technology work in the school portfolio for design and technology.

Strategies for the language co-ordinator

▌ liaise with the design and technology co-ordinator to plan appropriate links on a whole school basis
▌ liaise with the design and technology co-ordinator in providing appropriate teaching resources, e.g. non-fiction texts, stories linked to design and technology units of work, writing frames suitable for use in design and technology
▌ create a folder of examples of children's work from different subjects, including design and technology, that show examples of different types of language.

Strategies for the class teacher

▌ plan opportunities to develop language through design and technology activities
▌ be aware of opportunities for reading and writing texts related to design and technology in the literacy session, e.g. instructions, explanatory texts, playscripts related to puppets the children have made
▌ collect examples of fiction and non-fiction texts related to the design and technology units of work you teach
▌ provide opportunities for children to publish examples of their language work in design and technology, e.g. class big books, sets of instructions for other children to use
▌ when preparing worksheets to support children's thinking in design and technology, consider the language requirements as appropriate
▌ prepare resources for children to use in design and technology that encourage

reading and writing for a real purpose
▌ label a display showing the language and design and technology that has been developed
▌ make the links explicit to the children and help them to apply learning from one situation to the other, e.g. talk about the parallels between writing for a particular audience and designing for a particular user, remind them of how to use contents, index and key words when researching in design and technology, encourage the use of correct sentence structure when writing about what they did in design and technology
▌ include suitable examples of language work carried out in a design and technology context in children's individual language portfolios
▌ encourage the children to use language appropriately in design and technology, e.g. using accurate vocabulary, making quick notes when designing, writing in an appropriate style for a particular audience or purpose
▌ ensure that the children are aware of the links and understand what particular aspect of language they are focusing on.

3.3   Strategies for long, medium and short term planning

When planning either the language or the design and technology curriculum, the objectives need to be clearly identified. It is possible to identify language objectives in a design and technology scheme of work, and to show how design and technology can be developed in a language session.

Strategies for long term planning by the language and design and technology co-ordinator

▌ the language and design and technology co-ordinator should, if at all possible, liaise over the long term planning throughout the school
▌ using a chart, such as the one below, the co-ordinators should review what is already happening and then they can identify which focus/es would be most appropriate for

developing language through design and technology

Year Group	Language	Design and technology	History
Year 1 Autumn	Non-fiction writing: labels	Moving pictures mechanisms: put labels on drawing of moving picture	
Spring	Fiction reading; traditional rhymes/ playground chants	Playground structures: teach rhymes such as See Saw, Majorie Daw	
Summer			
Year 2 Autumn			
Spring			

each unit of work. The language co-ordinator could do this with other subjects to ensure that there is a balance of different types of language across the whole school and across the whole curriculum. Look at Chart A and Chart B on pages 39 and 44 for ideas.

If it is impossible for the two co-ordinators to get together, one of the co-ordinators could construct a chart (as above) and pass it to the other for comments. Remember that while every unit of work in design and technology involves language, not all aspects are appropriately developed through all units.

Strategies for medium term planning by year groups or individual teachers

▌ the next stage is to look at the language focus and identify whether it is best covered in investigative, disassembly and evaluative activities, focused practical tasks, and/or the design and make assignment
▌ depending on whether the language work will be carried out in the Literacy Hour or in the design and technology session, annotate the appropriate medium term planning sheets (see figures 1 and 2)
▌ again, look at Chart A and Chart B on pages 39 and 44.

Strategies for short term planning by the class teacher

When planning the individual activities, the class teacher will need to think about:
▌ the key objectives for each session
▌ teaching aids such as a large chart, a particular story book
▌ photocopiable support sheets for the children (see Section 5)
▌ classroom organisation, including how the children are to be grouped. For example, each group might need a confident scribe.

Figure 1 Medium term planning Year 3 Autumn Term Unit of Work Photograph frames			
Learning objectives	Possible teaching activities	Learning outcomes	Links to this unit Language: Word level work: make a glossary of words related to structures Text level work: record how they made their frame using a storyboard with drawings and captions

■ communication with other adult support to
ensure that they understand the key
language focus for the session.

Figure 2 Literacy Hour planning sheet		Year 5	Spring Term
Shared Reading/ writing	Shared word/ sentence/text	Guided/independent Group tasks	Plenary
Mon Biscuit making activity (D&T) NLS24 Discuss example of a written evaluation	Using prepared evaluation, examine use of effective nouns and verbs	Biscuit making activity (D&T) Groups 1 &2 Independent writing – evaluation of their biscuits Groups 3 &4 Guided writing use a framework	Recap on example. Go over structure and effective nouns and verbs using children's work
Tues			
Wed			

Section 4

Case studies

developing language through design and technology

Year 1
Unit of work:
Making a book
Gretel Roberts
Merridale Primary School,
Wolverhampton

> **Key language focus**

▌ fiction reading: stories with familiar settings
▌ fiction writing: writing a simple picture storybook with sentences

The children made their own fold over booklets, using various fastenings

> **Introduction**

Gretel Roberts is a design and technology co-ordinator in this urban primary school, minutes away from the town centre. It is a one form entry school with an attached nursery. Gretel has been on a 10-day co-ordinators' course which helped her to develop her own knowledge and understanding of design and technology and enabled her to lead the development of the subject in her school. She has written a policy and scheme of work and support for implementation has been through Inset days, twilight sessions and informal meetings. At Key Stage 1 fiction books were already a popular way of introducing design and make assignments and, with the introduction of the Literacy Hour, this has been extended to focusing on non-fiction texts for gathering information.

> **The teacher's intentions for the children**

▌ to create their own story book with a moving part
▌ to gain knowledge about joining and to use this knowledge to hold their book together
▌ to hear and re-enact a range of stories
▌ to be able to write their own story for the book which they make.

> **Stages of the project**

1. The children investigated, disassembled and evaluated a variety of books. They examined them to see how they were made, including how they were joined together. They discussed the stories, retelling them in their own words. Storyboards were used to help them to sequence their own stories, and pro formas of front covers enabled the children to model their books on a conventional one.

2. The children investigated sliders, hinges and different joins. They made their own fold over booklet with a moving part, trying different hinges and joiners to see which worked best.

3. Following on from the stories the children had read and re-enacted, they decided upon a story they wanted to write. They designed the story, using a storyboard. They decided upon the type of hinge which they would use for their book and one part which would move.

4. They evaluated the books by reading them to each other and to other classes. They could see which books were strong and stayed together well; which stories were enjoyed by others; and which moving parts worked well.

> **Drawing out the language**

▌ fiction: reading comprehension and writing composition

developing language through design and technology

The children read, and had read to them, a variety of stories, which they then retold and re-enacted through role play and the use of puppet shows. They wrote their own stories, based on stories which they had read and had read to them.

⟹ **Other aspects of language which were developed included:**

▌ speaking and listening

The children listened to each others' stories and used a variety of voices and styles when speaking for their puppets.

▌ sentence construction and punctuation

When writing their stories, the children were encouraged to think about appropriate grammar and to write in sentences.

▌ vocabulary extension

The children created a class collection of words which included story book, puppet, mechanism, hinge, join, joiner and strongest.

▌ technical vocabulary from the literacy strategy

Author; character; fiction; illustrator; layout.

⟹ **Evaluating the project**

The motivational factor for the children of making their own books was high and the story writing was in almost every case the best that the children had ever produced.

The finished product

The children could see a purpose for learning about different hinges and joiners and how important it was to choose strong ones for their books.

They wanted to practise their reading so that they read their books well to others.
To build on this project, the children's knowledge of mechanisms and joiners can be extended together with the use of a wider range of materials.

⟹ **Developing further the links between language and design and technology**

▌ pay more attention to identifying different types of stories and poems, particularly from a range of cultures

▌ examine the language which is used so that it can be used in their own stories

▌ compare and contrast stories and poems, identifying different settings, likes and dislikes

▌ build up simple profiles of different characters from stories and write about them

▌ identify a list of suitable stories, from those you have in school, to save time when planning the activity.

⟹ **Tips from teacher to teacher**

▌ The children do need to be able to cut paper neatly so I made sure that the children were given different cutting activities to develop this skill.

▌ I did find it worth while spending time on IDEAs especially examining a range of books. It was time consuming but I am sure that the end results were better because of this.

▌ If possible, have another adult on hand when the making takes place or have a circus of activities planned, only one of which is making.

▌ Be ready to remind the children that they have met some of the criteria for making their book e.g. it is bright, the story is interesting, the moving part works. If their book falls apart, it is worth spending time to repair it, perhaps in a class session, to overcome the disappointment and to help children to realise that modifications are often necessary.

developing language through design and technology

Year 2
Unit of work:
Vehicles
Carol Martin & Helen Marron,
St Nicholas R C Primary
School, Birmingham

⟩⟩⟩ Key language focus
Non-fiction reading and writing: instructions

⟩⟩⟩ Introduction
Carol Martin is IT and design and technology co-ordinator of a medium sized voluntary aided catholic primary school on the northern edge of Birmingham. Design and technology has developed well over the last two years due to much hard work, staff Inset training and financial support for materials. Classroom assistants and parents are often used to support design and technology and are well briefed as to the learning outcomes of each session. With the recent focus on literacy, Carol did not want to lose the momentum in the development of design and technology and immediately began to identify and extend the natural language links which were already in place in the scheme.

Helen Marron is deputy head and takes the Year 2 class. She has limited experience of design and technology but, with Carol's support, confidently delivered the unit of work and was thrilled with the quality of work that the children produced.

At work on the vehicle

⟩⟩⟩ The teacher's intentions for the children
❚ to understand how wheels and axles are fixed onto vehicles
❚ to be able to make a vehicle for a particular purpose, which moves
❚ to have experience of reading and writing instructions.

⟩⟩⟩ Stages of the project
1. The children investigated and disassembled a collection of wheeled toys to gain an understanding about wheels and axles and how and why they are used.

2. The children used construction kits to try out different ways of attaching wheels and axles to a chassis and to assemble different types of vehicles.

3. The children learnt how to measure and cut wood.

4. The children thought about the vehicle that they would make. They discussed its purpose and how they were going to attach the wheels and axles to the chassis so that they would turn round. They identified ways of finishing the model, made a simple flowchart to show the sequence of tasks and listed the materials and equipment that they would need.

5. Having made their model, they evaluated it against their original criteria.

⟩⟩⟩ Drawing out the language
❚ non-fiction reading and writing instructions
As a whole class activity, the children read and analysed a completed chart to show how to make a vehicle with a construction kit. This gave them a model for their own work. Before the children moved on to make their vehicle, they completed flow charts to show, step by step, the order in which they would make their vehicle. The children wrote the instructions in appropriate language and then put their own drawings in the boxes to support the text.

⟩⟩⟩ Other aspects of language which were developed included:
❚ speaking and listening
A class discussion provided opportunities for them to generate, explore, develop and clarify the children's

developing language through design and technology

ideas about their vehicle. They commented on which type of vehicle they would make and why they wanted to make it. One child had recently arrived from Turkey and wanted 'to make a bus like they have in Turkey so everyone will know what the buses are like in Turkey'. They talked about what components they would use for wheels and whether the wooden wheels or cotton reels were the right shape and size for their vehicle. Before writing their evaluations, the children were asked to give two reasons for their choices and to say if they would change their choices now. They were encouraged to listen to each other's reasons and comment on them.

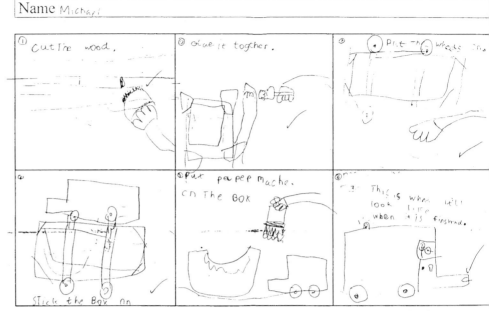

Name Michael

① Cut the wood.
② Glue it togther.
③ Put the wheels on
④
Stick the Box on
⑤ Put paper mache on the box
⑥ This is what it will look like when it is finished.

Chart showing step by step instructions for making the vehicle

■ vocabulary extension
The children built up individual collections of significant words e.g. vehicle, wheel, axle, design.
■ technical vocabulary from the Literacy strategy Evaluation, flow chart.

▷ **Evaluating the project**
The children were successful at recording tools/materials needed in list form. They had a clear idea of the sequence of tasks needed to complete the DMA.

The children were highly motivated and proud of their outcomes.

The designing was successful because of the input before they started to think about their own vehicle. The worksheets supported this.

Covering the boxes with paper was time consuming. Next time we will turn the boxes inside out and add finishes onto that surface.

The focus for the DMA was wheels and axles and this could have been achieved by just using boxes, not a wooden frame.

Developing further the links between language and design and technology
■ show the children different ways of writing and presenting instructions e.g. food unit, recipe as a numbered set of instructions

■ use the work of this unit as a focus for work on dictionaries and glossaries
■ make up some cards to use with the construction kits to show a sequence of how to make a vehicle
■ get the children to make up their own instruction cards to show how to make a model using a limited number of pieces of construction kit.

▷ **Tips from teacher to teacher**
■ keep a collection of wheeled vehicles together for this unit and work in science. It will save time trying to find suitable ones.
■ plan in the literacy before tackling the unit and adjust the design and technology IDEAS and FPTs accordingly. For example, the work on instructions in the Literacy Hour needs to come before the children write their plan for making.
■ don't be afraid to set up investigation

activities. We found that they were essential to the children's success with the DMA.
■ establish homework links. Activities could include collecting pictures of different vehicles and labelling them, looking at vehicles near the home and recording on a chart what the children have seen, and making an instruction sheet for something made at home.

developing language through design and technology

Year 2
Unit of work:
Playgrounds
Angy Burn,
Gastrells Primary School,
Stroud, Gloucestershire

➤ Key language focus
▌ non-fiction writing: letters
▌ speaking and listening

➤ Introduction
Gastrells is a newly built semi rural school with extensive grounds. It has seven classes and a Language Centre, which provides support for those with language impairment from around the county. Angy has been science and technology co-ordinator for 11 years and runs Inset for Gloucestershire SATRO on a regular basis. Design and technology is well established and some classroom support is available from governors and parents. This project was submitted for the Primary Challenge, run by Gloucestershire SATRO.

➤ The teacher's intentions for the children
▌ to create their own model playground, having investigated a real one
▌ to develop their ability to work in groups
▌ to understand how to write a letter for a real purpose.

➤ Stages of the project
1. A visit to a local playground was made to investigate the layout of the area, the equipment and the users. Pre-prepared questions helped focus the children's judgements and adults acted as scribes.

2. In mixed ability groups of four, the children decided on a theme for their play area and drew initial designs. One child, acting as a scribe, drafted and re-drafted a letter to the Council, expressing their opinions as users of the current play area and submitting their ideas for change. They word processed the letters.

3. As an IDEA activity, each child made a piece of playground equipment out of Meccano and these were evaluated by the class.

4. The children revisited the play area to gather specific information about:
▌ what children like to do when they go to a play area
▌ the different sorts of movement that can be seen
▌ how structures are strengthened and stabilised
▌ what safety features were in evidence.

5. The children learnt about different sorts of mechanisms which allow movement e.g. swinging, rotating, moving up and down, balancing, through a combination of direct teaching, investigations with construction kits and toys, and trying out different constructing techniques.

6. Children investigated different types of materials and methods of joining and fastening and displayed results on prompt boards so that others could share the information.

7. Design and make assignment. In groups of four, the children had to design and make a themed play area. The group decided on the theme and what piece of equipment each person should make. Additional features were to be added after the play equipment had been made.

Designs were discussed with an adult and evaluated for feasibility and suitability for the task. Materials

---

Gastrells Primary School,
Kingscourt Lane,
Stroud,
Gloucestershire.
GL5 3PS

Dear Sir or Madam,
We have been thinking about the Rodborough Parish Council play area in Kingscourt Lane. We've been thinking about how to improve it. We went to look at it and we thought it was quite safe but it hasn't got much of a theme. We made up a good theme. We were doing about the story of Hansel and Gretel. We thought it would be good to have a theme about Hansel and Gretel. We

it would be scary to have a of a witch but we thought it be okay to have a model of and Gretel. We are going to Hansel and Gretel house stic sweets for stepping a rope swing with a wooden d the bottom of the axe in int. Hansel and Gretel and ....ger bread man models and wooden fire painted.
Yours faithfully
Jeremy Free
Cheryl Pitt
Stevie Nash
Lucille King

The letter the children wrote, and the local council's response

---

RODBOROUGH PARISH COUNCIL

F. A. Howarth
(Clerk)

FROME HOUSE,
BATH ROAD,
STONEHOUSE,
GLOS. GL10 2JS

Telephone: 01453 825956
27 March

Dear Stephen,

KINGSCOURT PLAY AREA

The Parish Council at their Meeting on 20 March were very impressed with the Project Work which you had undertaken inconnection with the Kingscourt Play Area.

They felt you should be congratulated for the amount of time effort and thought you had put into the Project.

Members of the Parish Council would welcome the opportunity of seeing the models you have prepared and I shall await hearing from you as to when this will be convenient.

From the Parish Council point of view, it might well be that they will take up the suggestion that the Play Area should be improved as their Project. If they do I will let you know.

Yours sincerely

F. A. Howarth

were identified; products were made and finished according to the group's theme; and products were evaluated against the original purpose for them.

➤ Drawing out the language

❚ non-fiction writing: letters

As a class, the children were shown how to write a letter to a person they did not know. They discussed the type of language which they should use, as well as the layout and the conventional start and finish. Then in small groups the children drafted and re-drafted their letters before sending them off.

➤ Other aspects of language which were covered included:

❚ speaking and listening

There were various opportunities to talk for a range of purposes. The children talked to adults in the play area and told them their opinions and judgements about the park; they discussed in small groups their ideas, taking turns to speak; they listened to others' opinions with regard to the theme which they should choose and they prepared a short presentation and spoke to the judges at the Primary Challenge day.

❚ vocabulary extension

The children collected words which particularly interested them e.g. equipment, playground, mechanisms, joining, movement, rotate, up and down, side to side.

❚ technical vocabulary from the Literacy strategy Fact, notes.

➤ Evaluating the project

The children had the opportunity to work in groups and the mixed ability grouping, in the main, worked well.

The children were really motivated to write their letters to the Council as they had a real purpose and were thrilled to receive letters in return. The project supported work relating to citizenship as the children saw that people in authority listened, respected and responded to their view point.

Presenting their work to a panel of judges at the annual Primary Challenge helped them to organise their work and to report it in a structured way.

To find sufficient time for the project, some activities were done in language time and some in mathematics and this worked well.

The children have a sound understanding of how some mechanisms work, which can be built on in their Key Stage 2 work.

➤ Developing further the links between language and design and technology

❚ ensure that all staff are familiar with the Literacy framework before we make more specific links

❚ get the co-ordinators working together to plan a whole school approach

❚ try to develop more materials/buy published ones that help to develop the links and have Inset in the use of them.

➤ Tips from teacher to teacher

❚ It would have been difficult to do so much preparatory work without the support of other adults.

❚ Explain to the children what the whole project is about at the start; this certainly helped them to be clear about their intentions.

❚ Having a good understanding of different sorts of mechanisms through FPTs allowed the children to design and make a variety of equipment with confidence.

❚ The 'prompt boards' (teaching aids) really helped the children to gain knowledge and understanding of joining and materials.

❚ By creating a book, using the children's ideas and opinions scribed by an adult, they were able to read and re-read comments which reinforced the design and technology process.

developing language through design and technology

Year 4
Unit of work:
Shadow puppets
Gillian Sheraton,
Abingdon Road Junior School,
Middlesborough

Key language focus
▮ speaking and listening: talking for a range of purposes
▮ fiction writing: collaborative writing

Introduction
Abingdon Road Junior school is situated in an inner city location and serves an established tightly knit community of mainly Punjabi speaking families, so the support from the Multicultural and Language Centres is widely used. Gillian is art and design and technology co-ordinator and has a class of 30 children to manage. The school gives particular priority to food and textiles, especially in a multicultural context. Parental help is encouraged so that particular skills can be shared throughout the community. Through careful planning in teams, the school makes use of cross curricular opportunities to deliver design and technology.

The teacher's intentions for the children
▮ to extend their knowledge and understanding of puppets and different ways of making them
▮ to design and make a large puppet
▮ to work collaboratively to write a play script and then perform it

Stages of the project
1. The children evaluated a range of puppets, including shadow ones, identifying how they moved, where they came from and when they would be used.

2. As a FPT, they made their own shadow puppets, exploring how they would get the joints to move and, in language, the children worked in small groups to create short stories, which they performed with their puppets.

3. The children were then introduced to the design and make assignment which was to make a puppet which was a metre tall. The puppets were to be made in groups and it was suggested that the children might use papier-mâché for the head – a technique which they had used previously. This would enable the children to give the puppet 3-D features.

4. Obviously, before the children could design the puppets, they needed to identify a purpose for them. It was suggested that they create a storyline, using well known characters. The children were given time for discussion in small groups and they knew that they had to come up with a short storyline after 20 minutes. Then they would vote for one. The result led to the adoption of characters from both the school and from Coronation Street, and each group chose a different character to make.

5. The children were encouraged to observe their chosen characters closely and make notes and drawings detailing appearance, dress and mannerisms.

6. Evaluation of the puppet construction and of what the characters would do and say was ongoing throughout the process. The problem of how to get the puppets to move was solved by the smallest child suggesting that the children hide behind the puppets and manipulate them that way.

7. The final evaluation came when the children performed the whole play to the school.

Drawing out the language
▮ speaking and listening
The work with puppets enabled the children to have varied opportunities to talk for a range of purposes which included talking to a live audience.

developing language through design and technology

As they practised the voices for their characters, they realised that they would have to speak with a Lancashire accent and use appropriate phrases if they had a character from Coronation Street. 'Howway the lads' was definitely not a Jack saying! This led to discussions about Standard English and how speakers adapt their vocabulary, tone, pace and style to suit different situations and audiences. The children used improvisation when they performed with their shadow puppets and appreciated the difference in the language that was used, when they moved on to a scripted play with the large scale puppets. They needed to express themselves clearly and confidently when they performed the play to the school and realised that they needed to project their voices in a large space.

▌writing composition

The script was definitely a group effort and certainly developed the children's team working skills. Each group worked out the storyline by brainstorming and then refining ideas and by drafting and redrafting their work. The more able writers took on the roles as scribes but everyone contributed ideas and care was taken, often through appropriate intervention, to ensure that everyone was involved.

⟶ Other aspects of language which were developed included:

▌vocabulary extension
The children defined familiar

The children put on a play using the puppets they created

vocabulary in their own words, using alternative phrases and expressions.
▌technical vocabulary from the Literacy strategy
Discussion, playscript, voice.

⟶ Evaluating the project

The children gained much useful background knowledge about puppets which certainly helped them later when they designed their own.

The FPTs did help the children learn new ways of joining materials, some of which were used later on the full sized puppets.
The scripts that the children wrote were of a good quality, almost certainly because they were motivated by the context.

One of the highlights was the obvious strengthening of relationships, both between the children and between myself and the children, through the use of so much collaborative work.

The project has demonstrated how design and technology can act as the starting point for meaningful language based activity from which the children can experience a wide variety of aspects at first hand.

⟶ Developing further the links between language and design and technology

▌explore the use of CD-ROMs and sites on the Internet so the children can use these as a resource. They could scan texts and note key points of interest.
▌design a poster and programme for their play using appropriate language.

⟶ Tips from teacher to teacher

▌Don't be afraid to give the children time to experiment with materials and ways of movement. It is worth it.
▌Do put out a collection of materials which the children can use while they are designing so they can see what is available when they design their puppet.
▌Once the children are clear what they want to do, you can stand back for much of the time and be an 'advisor'. It gives time to observe and assess.

developing language through design and technology

Year 5-6
Unit of work:
Fabric covered box
Kate Bennington,
Parsons Down Junior School,
Thatcham, Berkshire

⮞ Key language focus
▮ non-fiction writing: instructional texts, making notes, evaluating their work

⮞ Introduction
Kate Bennington is a co-ordinator in a large junior school, in the growing town of Thatcham. She found the 20-day Inset courses that she attended very valuable in helping her and her colleagues to develop knowledge of design and technology. She has taught language and mathematics throughout the junior age range. Resources are good but difficulties can arise during practical work as there is limited space in the open plan school.

⮞ The teacher's intentions for the children
▮ to design and make a fabric covered container for a purpose
▮ to develop the children's ability to write instructions, to make notes and to evaluate their work

⮞ Stages of the project
1. The children investigated a variety of containers, looking at 'traditional' designs and stereotypes such as a ballerina on top of a jewellery box for girls, a Paisley printed sponge bag for men, why the containers were designed in the way they were and for whom they were intended.

2. The children made a detailed examination of one container and recorded their findings by drawing and labelling it.

3. Next the children examined a variety of fastenings. They discussed why different fastenings had been used on the containers, whether they worked well, and which worked best on different materials.

4. The children took apart containers that could be disassembled and looked at the different parts and nets. They drew one on isometric paper. It was a good opportunity to teach how to use the paper as the shapes involved were mainly cuboids with few complex shapes.

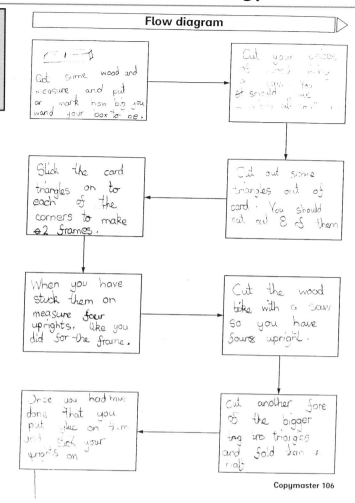

Flow diagram

Instructions on how to make a box

Copymaster 106

5. As a FPT the children were taught how to make a 3-D frame (they already knew how to make a 2-D one).

6. The children were shown how to draw, make and use a pattern to cover card shapes so that they could cover or line their container. They learnt to pad, to quilt using padding and to make neat corners by snipping the fabric across the corners and folding in the sides.

7. Design and make assignment
The children had to decide the purpose for the container they were to make. They decided on the covering/lining and used isometric paper to draw out what their intended container would look like. Before making the container, the children described the making process they were to undertake, recording their thoughts on a flow diagram in the form of a series of instructions. The children

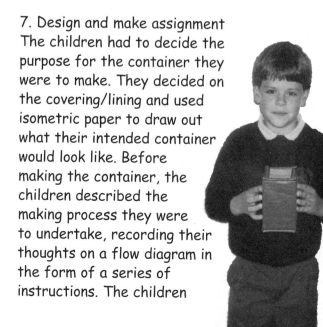

evaluated their containers by filling them with the articles for which the box was intended and using them. They wrote an evaluation using a writing frame.

⟫ Drawing out the language

▮ non-fiction writing composition

The children wrote out the instructions for making their containers, using a flow chart as a framework, and then tested the instructions when making the containers. The children were shown examples of leaflets and they discussed the language which had been used. It was simple, direct and written in the form of orders. They wrote up the notes that they made about a particular container into notes for others to read. They identified key points by numbering each one. They wrote up an evaluation of their work, using a framework.

⟫ Other aspects of language which were developed included:

▮ speaking and listening

During the investigation of the containers the children were given numerous opportunities to explore and explain ideas, to report and describe observations, to make reasoned and evaluative comments, presenting their thoughts to their peers. They listened to each other's ideas and responded to them.

▮ fiction: reading comprehension

The children read the Greek myth Pandora's box and then answered questions about the passage. This allowed the children to show higher order reading skills such as inference and deduction, offering opinions and expressing preferences based on the text that they had read.

▮ vocabulary extension

The following words were collected and used in spelling tests: container, user, function, three-dimensional, pattern, fray, quilting, padding, lining, covering, wadding.

▮ technical vocabulary from the Literacy strategy

Technical vocabulary, chronological sequence, plan.

⟫ Evaluating the project

All the children made a container and were able to identify an appropriate purpose for it.

The making of the 3-D framework proved very useful as the children were able to build on this knowledge when making their own containers.

The flow chart pro forma certainly helped the children to order their thoughts, particularly the special needs children, and provided a real context for instructional writing and testing it out.

The standard of the various forms of language that was used was generally high, almost certainly because the children could see the purpose for its use and the project generated much enthusiasm.

The framework for their evaluation helped the children to think about different aspects of it and to provide reasons for their thoughts.

⟫ Developing further the links between language and design and technology

▮ next time the project is undertaken, we could ask the children to give a short presentation about their research or their DMA.

▮ the children could write up their flow chart, to include modifications, into a leaflet form and another class could test out some; others could be read and evaluated for clarity.

⟫ Tips from teacher to teacher

▮ I would put the language based activities into the Literacy Hour. They fit the objectives to be covered, give a context for the work and free up time for specific design and technology objectives to be covered.

▮ Make sure that the children work through each step. Do get the children to note any changes that are needed. This prevents the children from being overloaded and pressured into rushing and making mistakes.

Some of the finished boxes on display

developing language through design and technology

Year 6
Unit of work:
A building suitable for a
green field site
Alison Hopton, Prestbury St
Mary's Junior School,
Prestbury

> **Key language focus**

■ non-fiction writing

> **Introduction**

Prestbury St Mary's is a village school which has a two form entry. As an established co-ordinator, Alison has been able to build up both staff's and children's confidence and expertise in design and technology. She has also worked outside her school, running INSET and working as part of the Gloucestershire core curriculum project team, so she has experience of looking at the links between design and technology and other subjects. This project was extensive and the FPTs and IDEAs activities were carried out over a period of time and built on work from the whole of Key Stage 2. However, some of the work was carried out in literacy sessions, thus maximising the time available. The links with a variety of outside agencies were very useful and provided the children with real life situations when they needed to speak, listen, read and write.

> **The teacher's intentions for the children**

■ to have the opportunity to try a variety of non-fiction writing, drawing on and extending the skills learnt from their whole primary education
■ to develop and use a range of making skills by producing a quality scale model of their building
■ to gain knowledge and understanding of the real world of planning and building

> **Stages of the project**

1. The children examined a green field site within the village, which included soil analysis, finding dimensions, and examining local documents to determine previous land usage.

2. A talk from a structural engineer from Westbury Homes focused on how the site might be developed.

3. Working in groups, the children collected and sorted their ideas and presented these to the other groups.

4. Each group produced a proposal booklet. Tight time constraints were used.

5. The proposals were talked through with the teacher and accepted. Some needed modifications.

6. The children made their scale models, drawing on skills and knowledge and understanding learnt previously in FPTs and IDEAs activities.

7. Evaluation took the form of a presentation to the whole year group, class teachers and a representative from Westbury Homes.

> **Drawing out the language**

■ non-fiction writing composition
Whilst the children used a range of composition, it is only possible to focus on one or two different types, perhaps those which the children are least confident with.
■ journalistic style
The children studied a variety of newspaper reports to gain knowledge of journalistic styles for different types of articles, before creating their own. The children said, "we are confident that the report on the following page is a positive replica of what newspapers really would think and write about Sub-sensation." The work provided a real context for the use of ICT, with children planning, drafting and editing their newspaper articles.

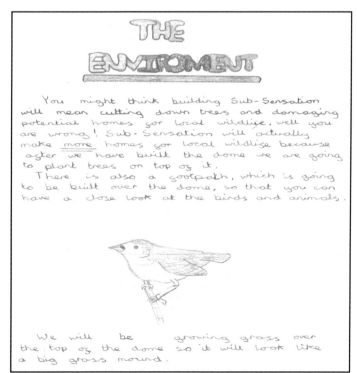

The children considered the environmental implications of building Sub-Sensation

➤ Other aspects of language which were developed included:

▌ writing

The children constructed an effective argument as to why there was a need for this new facility. They discussed negative reasons which might be put forward for the building, including environmental objections, and positive gains that such a facility would bring.

▌ writing a leaflet and a questionnaire

The children had to select the appropriate style and form to suit the audience.

▌ reading a variety of non-fiction texts (including CD-ROMs)

The children looked at texts which used different styles for different purposes.

▌ speaking and listening opportunities

Including brainstorming, listening to an outside speaker, presentations and questioning peers and adults.

▌ vocabulary extension

They built a bank of useful terms and phrases for argument such as whereas, nevertheless, by comparison.

▌ technical vocabulary from the Literacy strategy

Journalistic writing, viewpoint, synopsis.

➤ Evaluating the project

The project takes advantage of the natural and exciting links between, in particular, a range of writing opportunities and design and technology.

Certainly, the work on the FPTs throughout the year was time well spent as the children did apply the knowledge and skills that they had learnt to produce good quality models. A more rushed approach may have meant poor quality finishes.

The involvement of the outside agency and other adults certainly gave the children useful opportunities to gain confidence in asking questions.

➤ Developing further the links between language and design and technology

▌ the staff intend to plan a more organised approach to linking language and design

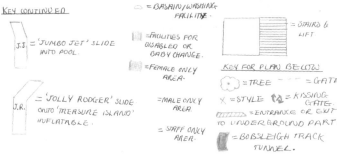

KEY CONTINUED

J.J. = 'JUMBO JET' SLIDE INTO POOL.

J.R. = 'JOLLY RODGER' SLIDE ONTO 'TREASURE ISLAND' INFLATABLE.

= BASIN/WASHING FACILITIE.

= FACILITIES FOR DISABLED OR BABY CHANGE.

= FEMALE ONLY AREA.

= MALE ONLY AREA.

= STAFF ONLY AREA.

= STAIRS & LIFT.

KEY FOR PLAN BELOW

= TREE   = GATE

X = STYLE   = KISSING GATE

= ENTRANCE OR EXIT TO UNDERGROUND PART.

= BOBSLEIGH TRACK TUNNEL.

Oblique view of outside ✗ Not to scale

The dome.

Rest of field

Bridge

in / out

and technology (and numeracy) throughout the school. Planning has to be tight, with objectives identified on the literacy and/or the design and technology planning sheets. The design and technology planning sheets, in future, will contain an area specifically for planning and recording the links, including references to the literacy framework.

➤ Tips from teacher to teacher

▌ Identify well in advance your FPTs and teach these throughout the year, allowing the children to draw on these skills during the project.

▌ Mixed gender groups worked well for this project.

▌ Allow children time to develop their ideas.

▌ The project will run smoothly if the initial planning is right.

SUB-SENSATION

Section 5

Support materials

Opportunities for developing literacy through the design and technology National Exemplar Scheme of Work

These outline activities which can be linked to at word, sentence and text level for each unit of work in the National Scheme. Whilst it is accepted that many schools may not be delivering all the units of work, the themes are commonly used and many ideas are easily transferable to other contexts.

Supporting specific literacy objectives through design and technology activities

These charts show ways of enhancing termly literacy objectives through design and technology. A literacy objective is given and one example of a design and technology activity, which can support it, is detailed. Other possibilities are outlined to give teachers a range of possibilities on which to draw.

Photocopiable sheets

This section contains a range of photocopiable sheets which can be used in the Literacy Hour, a language session or a design and technology session across Key Stages 1 and 2. The sheets link with each term's literacy objectives as well as other aspects of language. The design and technology content is linked with the National Scheme of Work, as many schools are adopting this and the contexts are ones with which schools are familiar. If there is an obvious 'best fit' place for them this is indicated, for example 'this sheet should be used in the introductory section of the Literacy Hour with the whole class', but otherwise it is left to the user to decide when it would be most appropriate to use them. There are brief notes about the suggested use of each sheet at the end of the section. The sheets themselves are without additional decoration for a number of reasons:

▪ decoration can obscure the main objectives for the sheet and children can spend much time, for example, just colouring in

▪ the illustrations may make the sheets unsuitable for a particular group of children

▪ the user may want to add additional items, including his/her own decoration.

developing language through design and technology

Opportunities for developing literacy through the design and technology National Exemplar Scheme of Work

1A   Moving pictures
Word level work:
∎ reading labels, naming tools and equipment
∎ making collections of words related to tools and equipment, materials and moving parts, e.g. slider, slot.

Sentence level work:
∎ writing captions to accompany moving pictures
∎ using a sequence of drawings with labels and captions to plan story telling.

Text level work:
∎ responding to stories and rhymes
∎ reading and sharing books with moving parts
∎ using moving pictures to re-tell a story
∎ making simple lists for planning
∎ reading and following simple instructions.

1B   Playgrounds
Word level work:
∎ reading labels, naming tools and equipment
∎ making collections of words related to playgrounds, e.g. ladder, climb, swing.

Sentence level work:
∎ using capital letters when writing sentences describing their work.

Text level work:
∎ reading and learning playground chants and rhymes
∎ using non-fiction books to find out more about playgrounds
∎ writing questions for a survey about play activities
∎ writing labels for drawings showing an existing playground or their ideas for new possibilities.

1C   Eat more fruit and vegetables
Word level work:
∎ reading labels, naming equipment
∎ making collections of words related to tools and equipment, names of fruit and vegetables and words to describe their characteristics, e.g. juicy, mushy
∎ words to describe parts of fruit and vegetables, e.g. pip, leaf, stalk, peel.

Sentence level work:
∎ writing captions to accompany display of fruit and vegetables.

Text level work:
∎ reading poems about food
∎ using a range of non-fiction books and comparing them
∎ writing a simple recount of their designing and making.

1D   Homes
Word level work:
∎ reading labels, naming tools, equipment and materials
∎ making collections of words related to homes, e.g. building, roof, bricks, windows.

Sentence level work:
∎ writing captions to accompany model homes.

Text level work:
∎ looking for references to homes in stories and poems
∎ writing their own questions before searching for information
∎ using non-fiction books about homes and other texts, e.g. estate agent details
∎ labelling drawings
∎ making a class book about homes using language and features of non-fiction texts, e.g. labelled diagrams, captions for pictures.

2A   Vehicles
Word level work:
∎ reading labels, naming equipment and materials
∎ making collections of words related to mechanisms, e.g. vehicle, wheel, axle, spacer.

Sentence level work:
∎ writing captions to display with models and other work.

Text level work:
∎ using non-fiction texts to find out about different types of wheeled vehicles
∎ reading simple written instructions
∎ writing and drawing instructions using the appropriate structure and style of language to explain to others how to make a wheeled vehicle
∎ reading poems and stories related to vehicles.

2B   Puppets
Word level work:
∎ reading labels, naming equipment and materials related to textiles

developing language through design and technology

■ making collections of words related to textiles, e.g. felt, sew, needle, glue.

Sentence level work:
■ investigating other ways of presenting texts for their puppet plays, e.g. speech bubbles
■ using commas when writing lists of materials.

Text level work:
■ writing a list of criteria for their puppets
■ reading stories and poems from other cultures
■ using texts for ideas, e.g. characters, events, description of appearance
■ writing character profiles for their puppets
■ re-telling stories in groups.

2C   Winding up
Word level work:
■ reading labels naming equipment and materials
■ making collections of words related to mechanisms, e.g. wheel, axle, winch, handle.

Sentence level work:
■ using commas when writing lists of tools, equipment and materials needed.

Text level work:
■ re-telling stories or rhymes in groups
■ using the language of time, e.g. first, after, while, when writing an account of their designing and making
■ using annotated drawings to show information about their designs for winding up toys.

2D   Joseph's coat
Word level work:
■ reading labels, naming equipment and materials
■ making collections of words related to textiles, e.g. fabrics, needle, glue, pattern.

Sentence level work:
■ using commas when writing lists of materials needed
■ using sentences correctly when writing about their work.

Text level work:
■ reading traditional stories
■ discussing the events in a story and the language used to describe characters' feelings
■ producing a flow chart to explain their process of designing and making
■ writing a review of their work.

3A   Packaging
Word level work:
■ making collections of words related to packaging, e.g. net, score, tab, cuboid, pyramid
■ using the context to infer meaning of unknown words when reading text on packaging.

Sentence level work:
■ using sentences correctly when writing about their work.

Text level work:
■ analysing types of text found on packaging
■ reading and following simple instructions, e.g. for constructing a net
■ using a matrix to record notes on different types of packaging investigated
■ writing text in appropriate form, style and presentation for their own packaging
■ using ICT to bring the text for their packaging to a published form experimenting with layout, font and use of upper and lower case lettering.

3B   Sandwich snacks
Word level work:
■ making collections of words related to foods and their sensory characteristics to help children in their evaluation of food products, e.g. names of different bread products, words to describe texture of foods such as chewy, crisp, smooth.

Sentence level work:
■ experimenting with adjectives to compose a short advertisement for their sandwich snack.

Text level work:
■ writing recipes for their sandwich snacks drawing upon their experience of analysing instructional texts
■ writing a non-chronological report about the different types of sandwich snacks investigated
■ using simple flowcharts to plan their work.

3C   Moving monsters
Word level work:
■ making an on-going dictionary of D&T terms including those related to tools and equipment, materials and components, e.g. pneumatics, tubing, plunger, pivot, connection.

Sentence level work:
■ using words and phrases that signal time sequences when writing about their work.

developing language through design and technology

Text level work:
- reading stories and poems about monsters
- using texts for ideas, e.g. characters, description of appearance
- writing poems or stories based on monster characters created
- reading and following simple instructions
- using annotated drawings to explain how their design will work.

3D   Photograph frames
Word level work:
- making a glossary of words related to structures, e.g. stable, strengthen, reinforce.

Sentence level work:
- using commas when writing lists of materials needed
- using words and phrases that signal time sequences when writing about their work.

Text level work:
- using a grid for making notes about different examples of photo frames investigated, e.g. recording information about materials, possible users, shape, method of decoration, method of making stable
- generating ideas through brainstorming
- recording how they made their frame using a storyboard with drawings and captions.

4A   Money containers
Word level work:
- making an on-going dictionary of D&T terms including those related to tools and equipment, materials and components, e.g. textiles, pattern, template, fastening.

Sentence level work:
- understanding the use of past, present and future tenses when writing about their work at different stages of their designing and making.

Text level work:
- reading and following instructions
- writing clear instructions using conventions learned from analysing texts
- using annotated drawings to explain how their design will work
- collecting information from investigating a variety of money containers and presenting it as a bank of ideas with drawings and notes.

4B   Storybooks
Word level work:
- collecting words related to work on mechanisms, e.g. rotary and linear movement, lever, linkage, pivot
- using the appropriate form of handwriting for different tasks within the unit, e.g. for presenting final text or making notes.

Sentence level work:
- using adjectives and adverbs effectively in their story writing.

Text level work:
- collaborating with others to write a story with a particular audience in mind
- using different ways to plan a story, e.g. brainstorming, notes, diagrams
- planning a story in sections
- exploring narrative order: identifying and mapping out the main stages of the story: introductions – build ups – climaxes or conflicts – resolutions, and using these stages to identify moving features
- making notes to help in planning jobs to be done, allocating tasks and keeping a record of what has been achieved.

4C   Torches
Word level work:
- collecting words related to work on electrical control, e.g. switch, battery, connection, wire strippers, insulating, conducting, component.

Sentence level work:
- using tenses correctly in writing to explain how a particular torch works.

Text level work:
- reading and following instructions
- writing clear instructions using conventions learned from analysing texts
- using annotated drawings to explain how their design will work
- designing an advertisement for their torch.

4D   Alarms
Word level work:
- collecting words related to work on electrical control, e.g. switch, battery, connection, wire strippers, insulating, conducting, component.

developing language through design and technology

Sentence level work:
▌ using tenses correctly in writing about how an alarm system works.

Text level work:
▌ reading and following instructions on ways of making different switches
▌ making notes to record group decisions and as a way of organising work
▌ using annotated drawings to explain how their design will work
▌ designing an advertisement for their alarm system.

5A   Musical instruments
Word level work:
▌ using alphabetic texts such as dictionaries and encyclopedias to find out about musical instruments and the correct terms to describe their component parts.

Sentence level work:
▌ using the imperative form when writing instructions.

Text level work:
▌ using a range of non-fiction texts to find out about musical instruments from a range of times and cultures
▌ making notes highlighting the key points from their reading
▌ writing a recount of a visit from a group of musicians demonstrating different types of instruments.

5B   Bread
Word level work:
▌ searching for, collecting and defining words related to bread, e.g. yeast, dough, knead, texture, consistency.

Sentence level work:
▌ using nouns, pronouns and verbs effectively when writing about their work.

Text level work:
▌ reading and following recipes
▌ preparing for reading about bread by identifying what they already know and what they would like to find out
▌ locating information efficiently using a range of texts including ICT sources
▌ writing an explanation of how bread is made using conventions learned from analysing texts
▌ evaluating their own work.

5C   Moving toys
Word level work:
▌ making an on-going dictionary of D&T terms including those related to tools and equipment, materials and components, processes and knowledge, e.g. cam, prototype, flowchart, dowelling.

Sentence level work:
▌ developing understanding of how writing can be adapted for different audiences by making a provided text, such as an explanation of how a mechanism works, suitable for younger children.

Text level work:
▌ investigating toys by reading selected stories from a range of cultures and making notes about information they find
▌ evaluating a range of texts about toys, comparing the language used for different purposes, e.g. promotional material, health and safety information, catalogues
▌ writing a specification for their toy
▌ using annotated drawings to explain how their design will work.

5D   Biscuits
Word level work:
▌ making a collection of words used to describe the flavour, texture and appearance of biscuits, e.g. crunchy, crumbly, sweet, layered
▌ investigating a collection of expressions that have a food theme, e.g. half baked, too many cooks spoil the broth, to know which side your bread is buttered, one man's meat is another man's poison, to have your cake and eat it.

Sentence level work:
▌ developing understanding of how writing can be adapted for different audiences by making a biscuit recipe suitable for a different audience.

Text level work:
▌ reading and following instructions
▌ writing clear instructions using conventions learned from analysing texts
▌ comparing examples of instructional texts by looking at recipes from different sources and analysing the language and the way they are presented
▌ collecting information by making notes with text and drawings when reading biscuit recipes and investigating a variety of biscuits
▌ writing an evaluation of their work
▌ writing an advertisement for their biscuits using appropriate language.

developing language through design and technology

6A   Shelters

Word level work:

▌ making a collection of technical D&T terms including those related to structures, e.g. textiles, framework, reinforce, scale model, tension, rigid, flexible.

Sentence level work:

▌ using active and passive verbs appropriately in different forms of writing related to the project, e.g. specifying criteria for their shelters, describing what they will do, writing a summary of planning regulations.

Text level work:

▌ using a range of non-fiction texts to find information about different types of shelters

▌ making notes to support group designing and making

▌ annotating drawings at different stages of their deigning and making, e.g. to show their design ideas, to mark any modifications with the reasons why, evaluating their designs

▌ looking at official planning documents to identify characteristic features of the language used

▌ writing a balanced report on a proposed building development in the area.

6B   Slippers

Word level work:

▌ find out the correct terms for component parts of footwear

▌ investigate metaphorical expressions that use textiles as a theme, e.g. a stitch in time saves nine, to cut your cloth accordingly, coming apart at the seams, to lose the thread.

Sentence level work:

▌ making correct use of grammar and punctuation in writing related to the topic.

Text level work:

▌ writing letters to footwear manufacturers and retailers requesting information

▌ reading and following instructions

▌ writing specifications

▌ using annotated drawings to explain how their design will work

▌ planning their work in a step by step sequence.

6C   Fairground

Word level work:

▌ making an on-going dictionary of D&T terms including those related to electrical control and mechanisms, e.g. control, switch, insulation, pressure pad, worm gear.

Sentence level work:

▌ revising the language conventions and grammatical features of different types of text through writing within the unit, e.g. explanatory texts, instructional texts, discursive texts.

Text level work:

▌ using a range of fiction and non-fiction texts to inform their designing and making

▌ reading and following instructions

▌ using annotated drawings to explain how their designs will work

▌ writing a review of their work including changes made along the way and a final evaluation.

6D   Controllable vehicles

Word level work:

▌ making an on-going dictionary of D&T terms including those related to electrical control and mechanisms, e.g. control, switch, insulation, pressure pad, worm gear.

Sentence level work:

▌ revising the language conventions and grammatical features of different types of text through writing within the unit, e.g. explanatory texts, instructional texts, discursive texts.

Text level work:

▌ using a range of non-fiction texts to inform their designing and making

▌ reading and following instructions

▌ using annotated drawings to explain how their designs will work

▌ writing a review of their work including changes made along the way and a final evaluation.

When	Literacy objective	Example of a D&T activity	Other possibilities related to D&T
Year R	Pupils should be taught: to make collections of personal interest or significant words and words linked to particular topics (Word level – 11)	As part of a project on homes, the children went on a walk in the local area to look at different houses and to compare some of their features such as windows, doors, chimneys and roofs. The teacher and children compiled a list of words relating to parts of the houses and used this to help with ideas when designing and making model homes in groups.	■ making lists of tools and materials – matching words to pictures and real examples ■ making a collection of names of fruits during work with food ■ during a session on tasting fruits the teacher scribes words the children use to describe the characteristics of fruit, e.g. juicy, sweet, crunchy, mushy. The children match these words to drawings of the fruits
Year R	to use knowledge of familiar texts to re-enact or re-tell to others, recounting the main points in correct sequence (Text level – 7)	The teacher shows the children how to punch holes and use split pins to make simple moving pictures. The children practise this with drawings provided on photocopied sheets. The teacher and children choose some characters from a favourite story/song/poem and discuss how they can bring them to life through making simple moving pictures. The children use these moving pictures as props in their re-telling of the story.	■ making puppets to represent characters from a familiar song or rhyme ■ making models with construction kits to help in re-telling a story ■ making simple masks to use when acting out a story
Year R	through guided and independent writing: to write labels or captions for pictures and drawings (Text level – 12)	The teacher asks the children to draw a picture of their finished models. Through guided or independent writing the children write a caption to explain their drawing, e.g. 'I made a fire engine out of Mobilo. My fire engine has a ladder on top'.	■ making captions to go with a collection of products such as shoes, e.g. baby shoe – it is soft, wellington boot – good for splashing in puddles ■ adding labels to a drawing of a product, e.g. fire engine – wheels, ladder, where driver sits
Year R	to use writing to communicate in a variety of ways, incorporating it into play and everyday classroom life, e.g. recounting their own experiences, lists, signs, directions, menus, labels, greeting cards, letters. (Text level – 15)	The role play corner has been set up as a shop. The teacher and children have been talking about how a shop works and the different things you need to make it work. The teacher encourages the children to make things to go in the shop, to write signs and labels to display and to write shopping lists as part of their play in the shop.	■ writing a label to show where something is kept in the classroom ■ writing messages in greetings cards they design and make ■ working with the teacher to compile a list of things to do or things that will be needed when designing and making ■ writing party invitations or menus when working with food

When	Literacy objective	Example of a D&T activity	Other possibilities related to D&T
Year 1 Term 1	Pupils should be taught: to read and use captions, e.g. labels around the school, on equipment (Text level – 12)	The teacher has put up labels and captions in the activity area to show the names of tools and materials with illustrated tips on how to use them. During a focused practical task the teacher and children read together the captions and the teacher gives the children specific short tasks using the selected tools and materials.	■ reading safety rules together before starting work ■ using labels on boxes of materials to find what they need
Year 1 Term 1	to make simple lists for planning, reminding, etc. (Text level – 15)	As part of planning their work, the teacher shows the children the materials that are available and asks the children to write a list of what they will need to make their model playground. The teacher has labelled samples of the materials and tools for the children to use to help them.	■ the teacher and children compile a checklist together of 'Things to do' ■ the teacher and children discuss what the product they are designing and making will need to do to work well. The teacher writes up this list of criteria on the flipchart and refers to it at various stages of the designing and making. ■ making a list when discussing products, e.g. different things with wheels, different fruits, ways of eating fruits ■ making a list when discussing design decisions, e.g. What fillings could we have in our sandwiches? What do we need in our model playground?
Year 1 Term 2	to write labels for drawings and diagrams, e.g. growing beans, parts of the body (Text level – 22)	The children have been looking at a collection of shoes and talking about the different parts of the shoes and how they vary in terms of size, shape, materials and who would wear them. The children draw one of the shoes and label the component parts and any special features.	■ children draw a model they have made and label the component parts, the materials and any special features ■ children write captions for their model for a display of D&T work
Year 1 Term 2	to write simple questions, e.g. as part of an interactive display (Text level – 24)	As part of planning a class picnic the children write simple questionnaires to plan their own food and to send out with invitations to helpers and special guests, e.g. Which bread do you like – white bread, brown bread, white roll, brown pitta? Do you like ham, cheese or sandwich spread?...	■ writing questions as captions to go with a display of products, e.g. Which bag is the strongest? Which bag is the biggest? Which bag do you like best?
Year 1 Term 3	new words from reading and shared experiences, and to make collections of personal interest or significant words and words linked to particular topics (Word level – 8)	The teacher writes some words and phrases related to moving pictures on pieces of card, e.g. slider, up and down, slot, split pin. She uses these when showing the children examples of simple techniques. The teacher and children refer to these throughout the work, e.g. when labelling drawings and writing about how they made their moving pictures.	■ using the computer to collect words related to the unit of work ■ using a word bank related to the unit of work ■ having an on-going list of words in the classroom that children can add to, e.g. different wheeled vehicles, names of vegetables, names of parts of fruit
Year 1 Term 3	to identify simple questions and use text to find answers. To locate parts of text that give particular information including labelled diagrams and charts, e.g. parts of a car, what pets eat (Text level – 19)	As part of a D&T unit of work on homes children think about different types of buildings that people use for homes. They identify simple questions such as 'What are roofs made of?' and 'What are homes in other countries like?' The teacher supports children in using books to locate the information and encourages them to draw on this experience when designing and making their own model homes.	■ finding out about materials and products linked to their designing and making ■ using labelled posters to find out information, e.g. different types of fruit and vegetables

45

developing language through design and technology

When	Literacy objective	Example of a D&T activity	Other possibilities related to D&T
Year 2 Term 1	Pupils should be taught: to use language of time to structure a sequence of events, e.g. when I had finished..., suddenly..., after that... (Text level – 11)	Children record and review their designing and making by writing about how they designed and made a particular product. The teacher discusses the order of their work and the words and phrases that could be used to express time. She uses a writing frame with some of the children to support their thinking.	■ the teacher prepares a worksheet that has a set of familiar steps for making something jumbled up for the children to cut up and re-organise into the correct sequence. The children then present their work as a piece of text using the steps provided and connecting words to express time and sequence.
Year 2 Term 1	to write simple instructions, e.g. getting to school, simple recipes, plans, instructions for constructing something (Text level – 15)	As part of a project on toys children were asked to make a model of a moving toy using a limited number of pieces from a construction kit. The children produced a set of instructions with text and drawings so that another child could try to make the same model.	■ writing a recipe for a food product, e.g. a fruit dessert, a healthy sandwich, biscuits ■ following up a designing and making activity by producing a set of instructions for others to follow ■ making a 'how to...' class book where individual/groups of children present their work on instructions, e.g. how to cut a piece of wood, how to make a pop up card ■ using a set of instructions from a non-fiction book as a model for their own instructions
Year 2 Term 2	to prepare and re-tell stories individually and through role play in groups, using dialogue and narrative from text (Text level – 7)	Children design and make puppets to re-tell traditional stories from a range of cultures. They consider factors such as who will be using the puppet, what size it needs to be, how easy it will be to use and how it will represent the character.	■ children make props for re-telling a story incorporating some that use winches and pulleys ■ children use their knowledge of simple levers and sliders to make a 'read aloud' moving story book ■ children design and make masks using a range of materials to act out a story for class assembly
Year 2 Term 2	to read flow charts and cyclical diagrams that explain a process (Text level – 19)	Having explored a number of making techniques, the teacher discusses with the children how they might go about designing and making their own greetings cards. She discusses the different stages of working and records this in a flowchart on the flipchart. The teacher refers to the flowchart during and at the end of the children's making activity.	■ the teacher shows the children flowcharts and other process diagrams from non-fiction texts related to D&T, e.g. how bread is made ■ children record how to make something in a flowchart
Year 2 Term 3	to write non-fiction texts, using texts read as models for own writing, e.g. use of headings, sub-headings, captions (Text level – 20)	The children make a class book about designing and making moving vehicles. The children suggest different items that might be suitable for the book and the teacher reminds the children of other non-fiction texts they have read. They discuss together how to present their work.	■ children make a guide booklet to explain their display of D&T work ■ children make annotated drawings to show how a toy works and how it has been made using a text such as 'What's Inside? Toys' as a model
Year 2 Term 3	to write non-chronological reports based on structure of known texts, e.g. There are two sorts of x...; They live in x...; the A's have x ...; but the B's etc., using appropriate language to present, sequence and categorise ideas. (Text level – 21)	In a D&T unit of work focusing on food, children have investigated different types of fruit: their names, where they come from, their component parts (e.g. flesh, pips), their characteristics, ways of preparing them and what they might be useful for. Children write a report comparing types of fruit and how they might be used.	■ the teacher discusses a piece of children's writing that is a good example of how to structure a non-chronological report, e.g. results of an investigation into packed lunches ■ children compare different techniques for doing the same thing, e.g. attaching wheels and axles ■ children write about examples of stable structures that they have found in a walk around the school

46

developing language through design and technology

When	Literacy objective	Example of a D&T activity	Other possibilities related to D&T
Year 3 Term 1	Pupils should be taught: to collect new words from reading and work in other subjects and create ways of categorising them (Word level – 13)	During IDEAs and FPTs leading to children designing and making their own packaging, the teacher has kept an on-going word list. The teacher asks the children to organise these words into relevant categories such as shapes, tools, equipment, materials and processes.	■ children add new words learnt in D&T to their on-going dictionaries ■ children create a pictorial dictionary of D&T vocabulary
Year 3 Term 1	to write simple playscripts based on own reading and oral work (Text level – 14)	The teacher plans to link this literacy objective with a unit of work in D&T based on making glove puppets in textiles. The children work in teams to decide on the characters and to design and make the puppets for their story-telling activities.	■ children could create their own plays around how products might be used, e.g. a gift box they have made – Who is giving it? Who is receiving it? How do they feel when they first see it? What is inside it? What happens when they open it? What happens to the gift box afterwards? Is it used for something else? Doing this activity as part of designing can help children to identify what their product needs to be like and can help to stimulate ideas.
Year 3 Term 2	to write their own definitions of words, developing precision and accuracy in expression (Word level – 20)	Children create a glossary to describe words related to a particular D&T unit. These could be presented in appropriate ways, e.g. in bread shapes linked to a bread project.	■ the teacher gives the children a sheet with key words relating to a particular unit of work at the start of the unit. The children are asked to look out for those words and to think about what they mean. At certain points they are asked to add their own definitions. ■ the teacher and children look at glossaries in D&T related books. They discuss different features and when they might be useful, e.g. accompanying diagrams, different uses.
Year 3 Term 2	to read and follow simple instructions (Text level – 15)	Children follow a recipe for making bread as a focused practical task. The teacher and children read through the recipe and discuss the different parts and why it is in a particular order. They make the bread and evaluate it discussing with the teacher different ingredients that could be added to change the flavour or texture.	■ following instructions when working with construction kits ■ reading instructions to find out how to do a particular technique, e.g. making a pop up, doing tie dye ■ using non-fiction books to find out different ways of making something
Year 3 Term 3	to ensure consistency in size and proportions of letters and the spacing between letters and words (Word level – 18)	In a unit of work on designing and making greetings cards, the teacher plans a focused practical task on lettering. The children look at examples of different fonts, try out some and then select one that they practise before using it in their card. The teacher draws attention to aspects such as consistency in size, proportions of letters and spacing between letters, words and lines.	■ taking care in presentation where it is particularly important as in writing for an audience, e.g. writing thank you letters, producing captions for a display, designing and making a book for younger children
Year 3 Term 3	to write letters, notes and messages linked to work in other subjects ... selecting style and vocabulary appropriate to the intended reader (Text level – 20)	In preparation for a particular unit of work, the children were encouraged to consider the range of materials and products that would be useful. The children wrote letters home and to other members of the community to request some of the items that might be available as scrap resources or as items on loan.	■ children write 'Don't forget' messages to other members of their group or to themselves to help them to remember to bring in things from home or to do something in preparation for their designing and making assignment ■ children write invitations to an event they have organised, e.g. an exhibition of their work, a puppet show

developing language through design and technology

When	Literacy objective	Example of a D&T activity	Other possibilities related to D&T
Year 4 Term 1	Pupils should be taught: to define familiar vocabulary in their own words, using alternative phrases or expressions (Word level – 11)	As part of a project on money containers children collect terms related to working with textiles and make a glossary, e.g. seam, fray, pattern, tacking, interfacing	■ children could keep an on-going list of words and phrases with definitions in a D&T book. This could include tools, equipment, materials and processes. ■ teacher displays key technical vocabulary in a D&T unit of work and the children add definitions as the work progresses
Year 4 Term 1	to write clear instructions using conventions learned from reading (Text level – 25)	In a unit of work on food, children use a variety of books, magazines and the Internet to search for recipes for bread products. The teacher selects several examples that the children discuss in terms of structure, type of language used, level of detail etc. The children are asked to annotate a poor example of a recipe provided by the teacher with comments about how it could be improved. They are asked to present a recipe for the bread products they have designed and made at the conclusion of the project using what they have learnt about writing instructions.	■ writing instructions for designing and making a product ■ working in a group to produce a booklet of instructions on particular aspects of D&T for younger children, e.g. making simple pop ups, making biscuits, making a clay pot ■ looking critically at different examples of instructions, e.g. from construction kits, craft books, magazines, internet sites, recipe cards, video manual, "help" facility on the computer. Discussing issues such as audience, clarity, presentation, accuracy, level of detail, illustration.
Year 4 Term 2	to collaborate with others to write stories in chapters, using plans with particular audiences in mind (Text level – 12)	The teacher has planned a joint literacy and D&T project on 'Moving Story Books'. The children combine work on story planning and writing, audience and style of language with work on designing and making a book incorporating moving parts to bring the story to life. Having experimented with a range of techniques the children plan using a storyboard to identify sections of the story, illustrations and moving features and as a basis for allocating tasks within the group.	■ children follow up work on making puppets by changing genre from a play to a story ■ the teacher discusses with children the similar processes involved in planning and writing a story and designing and making a product in D&T. They identify the importance of considering the audience/user, ways of generating ideas, planning, evaluating, writing/making.
Year 4 Term 2	to identify from the examples the key features of explanatory texts: purpose, structure, language features, presentation (Text level – 20)	The teacher discusses with the children several examples of explanatory texts about a theme related to a D&T unit of work, e.g. how a torch works, different types of switches. They compare the similarities and differences between the examples and use what they have learned to present their own explanatory text.	■ children annotate an example of an explanatory text identifying key features ■ children make a class book about how things work using text and diagrams to explain the workings of familiar products
Year 4 Term 3	to use a range of presentational skills, e.g.: ■ print script for caption, sub-headings and labels ■ capital letters for posters, title pages, headings ■ a range of fonts and point sizes (Word level – 15)	The children use computer-generated text and handwriting and illustrations in presenting a group book about their D&T unit of work. They experiment using different fonts and point sizes and change the position of text and graphics by cutting and pasting on screen or re-arranging cut out pieces and using temporary fixings before making their final decisions.	■ children produce an advertisement for a product that they have designed and made, having analysed examples of advertisements to identify key presentational features and different possibilities ■ children focus on presentational skills when designing and making greetings cards ■ children investigate examples of packaging looking at the way that text is presented, e.g. different fonts etc.
Year 4 Term 3	to design an advertisement, such as a poster or radio jingle on paper or screen, making use of linguistic and other features learnt from reading examples (Text level – 25)	As part of a D&T unit of work on Healthy Eating, children have been looking at leaflets and posters encouraging people to eat more healthily. They have discussed issues such as why it is important to eat healthily, different food preferences and why some people might not eat healthily. They devise their own advertising campaign to promote healthy eating in the local community using a variety of media.	■ children analyse marketing material related to a product they are designing as part of a discussion on quality: what features are being emphasised, what is value for money, what image is being used to persuade consumers, who is the intended audience for the advertisement? ■ children design and make an advertisement promoting a product they have designed and made

When	Literacy objective	Example of a D&T activity	Other possibilities related to D&T
Year 5 Term 1	Pupils should be taught: to write instructional texts, and test them out (Text level - 25)	In pairs children write and draw instructions for making a simple moving model using gears from a limited number of construction kit components. They swap instructions with another pair and try to make the model. The children identify the strengths and weaknesses of the sets of instructions.	■ children write instructions for making an easily assembled product such as a fruit drink, a snack or an instant dessert mix and test out their instructions on other children ■ children write instructions for younger children to follow helping them to learn new techniques
Year 5 Term 1	to make notes for different purposes ... and to build on these notes in their own writing and speaking (Text level - 26)	Children investigate a collection of different photo frames thinking about users, materials, shapes, ways of making the frame stand up, ways of putting in photos and other design features. The children sketch different parts of the photo frames and make notes on interesting ideas that might be useful when designing and making their own.	■ recording notes from a group brainstorm ■ children make notes of design criteria that they can refer to throughout their process of designing and making including evaluating their final product ■ children add notes to their design sketches using different colour pens to show the different stages of their thinking, e.g. as a way of communicating ideas about what they will do, as comments on why they changed things, strong and weak points of their final product
Year 5 Term 2	to investigate metaphorical expressions and figures of speech from everyday life (Word level - 12)	As part of their work on textiles in D&T children collect everyday expressions related to textiles and discuss their origins and how well they explain ideas, e.g. to spin a yarn, to weave in and out, a stitch in time saves nine, to lose the thread.	■ collecting expressions that relate to other materials such as food or activities such as building and investigating their origins and meanings
Year 5 Term 2	to read a range of explanatory texts, investigating and noting features of impersonal style, e.g. technical vocabulary; hypothetical language; use of words/phrases to make sequential (Text level - 15)	Children used a CD-ROM such as 'The Way Things Work' to find out about different types of mechanisms. They printed out some sections of the text and analysed the language underlining specific features in different colours as directed by the teacher. They compared this with explanatory texts from other D&T sources.	■ children read extracts from other non-fiction texts related to D&T, e.g. books about materials such as clay, fabrics; a poster explaining how a product such as crisps is manufactured, magazine articles or promotional material about the development of new products; free leaflets about food products and food issues available from supermarkets
Year 5 Term 3	to select and evaluate a range of texts, in print or other media, for persuasiveness, clarity, quality of information (Text level - 14)	As part of a unit of work on moving toys the teacher gives children the opportunity to analyse the language used in advertising and comparing that with language used about the same subject in other contexts. Children evaluate texts from sources such as shopping catalogues, promotional material, packaging, consumer magazines and official health and safety information. The children write contrasting reviews of their toys from a range of perspectives using the appropriate language.	■ children evaluate texts related to other D&T units of work, e.g. texts related to food choices and healthy eating ■ children use the internet to search for websites that offer contrasting views of the same or similar products, e.g. websites of individual companies, retailers government bodies and sites aimed specifically at children. ■ children compare the clarity of texts explaining how to do things and use this to inform their own writing, e.g. recipe books, books on making techniques, instruction manuals
Year 5 Term 3	to draft and write individual, group or class letters for real purposes: to edit and present to finished state (Text level - 17)	As part of a general project on the local environment, children have evaluated the local play facilities. They have made a report of different people's views and have drawn up plans and models of possibilities for improved facilities within realistic constraints. They write letters to the local council sharing their findings and suggestions and inviting them to see the models and plans of their proposals.	■ children write thank you letters to a member of the local community who has helped them in their D&T, e.g. after a visit to a local factory or a visit from a parent who has shared their expertise in batik and tie dye ■ children write for information about a type of product that they are looking at in D&T, e.g. toys, footwear, snacks

developing language through design and technology

When	Literacy objective	Example of a D&T activity	Other possibilities related to D&T
Year 6 Term 1	Pupils should be taught: to write non-chronological reports linked to other subjects (Text level – 17)	Children write an evaluation of their performance in D&T. They consider various aspects such as their performance in designing and making, their ability to have ideas and share them with others, their ability to listen to other peoples' ideas, solve problems, finish work carefully and tidy up! They use examples of their work in different projects to write their own report.	■ children write a report about an investigation they have carried out as part of research leading to a designing and making assignment, e.g. the way electricity is used at a fairground, different sorts of indoor footwear across the world, an evaluation of different types of material suitable for making slippers
Year 6 Term 1	to use IT to plan, revise, edit writing to improve accuracy and conciseness and to bring it to a publication standard... (Text level – 18)	Children work in pairs and use the computer to plan and write an article about their current designing and making assignment for the school magazine.	■ children write articles for a special display of work or to publish on the school website ■ children use the computer to plan and edit clear instructions for others to follow ■ children write letters using the computer's facility for editing and revising text
Year 6 Term 2	to read and understand examples of official language and its characteristic features, e.g. consumer information, legal documents, headings, appendices and asterisks (Text level – 17)	As part of their work on 'Shelters' children are visited by a member of the local planning office who provides examples of official documentation that planners, builders and members of the public need to consider when planning a building project. The children use examples of text from these sources to develop understanding of official language and to inform their own design decisions when designing and making in groups.	■ children look at extracts from other sources of official documentation relevant to their D&T, e.g. consumer guidelines, health and safety guidance
Year 6 Term 2	to write a balanced report on a controversial issue, summarising fairly the competing views; analysing strengths and weaknesses (Text level – 19)	As part of a unit of work on Healthy Eating, children consider the food eaten at lunchtime in school. They examine the different views that children and others might have if school meals were made compulsory. They devise sample menus as an outcome of their practical designing and making activities.	■ writing balanced reports relating to issues in D&T, e.g. recycling arrangements in school, transport
Year 6 Term 3	to appraise a text quickly and effectively; to retrieve information from it; to find the information quickly and to evaluate its value (Text level – 17)	A teacher focuses on developing research skills in a D&T unit of work about bread. Children are reminded of information retrieval techniques and are given a time limit to work within. A wide range of sources are made available including books about food from around the world, recipe books, food magazines, material from organisations such as BNF and the Flour Advisory Bureau, promotional material and the Internet. Children work in groups to research specific aspects of the topic and use the Jigsaw technique to report back to the other groups. Children review their working process and the texts used. They use relevant information from their research when designing and making new bread products for a particular group of users.	■ children research other topics related to D&T units of work
Year 6 Term 3	to select the appropriate style and form to suit a specific purpose and audience, drawing on a knowledge of different non-fiction text types (Text level – 22)	Children work in groups to plan, produce and publish a non-fiction book about textiles that will be kept in the library for others to use. The children keep notes on ideas as they work through a unit of work in which they design and make slippers. They plan the contents of the book and make a mock up to show the layout of different sections. They use the computer, hand writing and illustrations including photographs to produce a book useful for the intended audience.	■ writing individual pieces of text in D&T units of work that are designed for a particular audience and use an appropriate form, e.g. an advertisement for a product, a letter to parents, text for a poster explaining how a selection of mechanisms work, a set of instructions, an article for the local paper ■ publishing books or other resources about different aspects of D&T for younger children to use

PHOTCOPIABLE SHEET 1

Fruit and vegetables

Name .... Date ....

Draw a circle round the words which tell us what your food looks like.
(Describe its appearance.)

red	white	yellow	green	brown	stripy
speckly	shiny	round	long	thin	fat
smooth	lumpy	soft	firm		

Draw a circle round the words which tell us what your food tastes like.
(Describe its taste and mouth feel.)

sweet	sour	juicy	crunchy	soft
sticky	watery	hard	firm	

Draw a picture of your fruit or vegetable here:

This is a ....

It is ....

Super salads

Name .... Date ....

I am going to make a .... salad.

I will use these foods: (ingredients)

....

....

....

....

I will use these tools: (equipment)

....

....

....

....

My salad looks like this:

Project title

Name .... Date ....

I am going to make a ....

I will use these materials:

....

....

....

....

....

I will use these tools (equipment):

....

....

....

....

....

Homes

Name .... Date ....

My model home is going to be for ....

It will have ....

I will use these materials:

....

....

....

....

....

I will use these tools (equipment):

....

....

....

....

....

My model house:

Homes

Name ....   Date ....

I saw this house when we went on a walk from school:

wall	door	window
chimney	roof	gate
garden	fence	hedge
stone	brick	wood
square	circle	rectangle
tall	small	big
inside	outside	porch
bungalow	flat	terrace

Vehicles

Name ....   Date ....

Draw your vehicle here and label all the parts. Give your drawing a title.

body	cab	chassis	axle
door	wheel	window	windscreen
headlight	number-plate	lorry	bus
trailer	fire-engine	car	ambulance

PHOTCOPIABLE SHEET 7

Vehicles

Name .... Date ....

Choose a box for the vehicle body	Fit the wheels to the axle
Choose (4) wheels	Decorate the body with paint or collage
How to make a vehicle	Make holes in the body for the axles
Stick the number plates on the front and back	

Bread

Name .... Date ....

Basic bread recipe

Ingredients
150 g flour
125 ml warm water
1 teaspoon yeast
$^1/_2$ teaspoon salt

Method
Weigh flour, put in bowl with salt.
Measure yeast, stir into flour.
Mix together to make a dough.
Sprinkle some flour onto table top.
Put dough onto it.
Knead dough for several minutes.
Shape the bread.
Grease tray or tin.
Put bread in warm place to rise.
Bake the bread.

Proving time: 30 minutes
Oven temperature: 200C or Gas Mark 7

Experimenting with different types of flour

Type of flour	Cost per 150 g	Appearance	Texture	Taste/flavour

Bread

Small group work

1. Collect information from the class or other groups of people, on:

    the amount of bread eaten per day/week
    when and how it is eaten
    the different types of bread preferred.

2. Represent the data collected in appropriate forms.

3. Research the importance of eating bread as part of a balanced diet.

4. Construct an argument in note form or full text, to persuade others that:

    'Bread is good for you – eat lots!'

5. Present the case to the class or a group.

PHOTCOPIABLE SHEETS

1. This sheet links with Unit of work 1c 'Eat more fruit and vegetables' and can be used to support NLS Year 1 Term 2 non-fiction writing. Once children have handled, examined and tasted fruit or vegetables, they can use the word bank to help them label their drawings and write simple sentences to describe the foods.

2. This sheet links with Unit of work 1c 'Eat more fruit and vegetables' and can be used to support NLS Year 1 Term 2 non-fiction writing. Using information from their own experience of tasting and handling fruit or vegetables, children can select and list appropriate foods and equipment for their chosen product. Some children may be able to write a simple non-chronological report of the activity or write their own recipe using a given recipe as a model.

3. This generic sheet can be used to support NLS Year 1 Term 2 non-fiction writing. Using information from their own experience of cutting, shaping and joining materials, children can select and list appropriate materials and equipment for their chosen product. Some children may also be able to write a simple non-chronological report of the activity.

4. This sheet links with Unit of work 1d 'Homes' and can be used to support NLS Year 1 Terms 2 and 3 non-fiction writing, making lists and writing simple sentences. Some children could go on to write an account of how they made their model.

5. This sheet links with Unit of work 1d 'Homes' and can be used to support NLS Year 1 Term 3 non-fiction writing. Children's investigative work on homes and buildings could also be used as the basis for a class book 'What we know about houses' incorporating labelled drawings and captions for pictures.

6. This sheet links with Unit of work 2a 'Vehicles' and can be used to support NLS Year 2 term 1 non-fiction writing. Children will need to have clearly labelled drawings as a basis for writing instructions for making their vehicle, which is shown on the next sheet.

7. This sheet links with Unit of work 2a 'Vehicles' and can be used to support NLS Year 2 Term 1 non-fiction writing. After children have made their model vehicle they can cut out the instructions on this sheet and re-arrange them in the correct order. This will give them a model for organising their own instructions sequentially which they can present either in writing or through labelled diagrams and drawings.

8. This sheet links with Unit of work 5b 'Bread' and can be used to support NLS Year 5 Term 2 non-fiction writing. Children can use the information they gather from the above experimentation to write a short report explaining the effects of using different flours when making bread.

9. This sheet links with Unit of work 5b 'Bread' and can be used to support NLS Year 5 Term 3 non-fiction writing. The activities in the Bread unit will often involve practical work in small groups. Meaningful and related work can be carried out by other groups using the suggestions above.

Section 6

Further reference material

Section 6 is is divided into two parts: publications aimed at teachers and those aimed at children. The lists are by no means exhaustive ones. The books have all been recommended by those who are in daily contact with children or who are involved with in-service training. As new books are constantly published, there is space left for you to add to these lists.

Publications aimed at teachers

Publications about developing language

Baddeley, G. (ed) (1992) Learning Together through Talk – Key Stages 1 and 2, Hodder & Stoughton

Bearne, E. (ed) (1998) Use of Language across the Primary Curriculum, Routledge

DfE (1995) English in the National Curriculum, HMSO

DfEE (1998) The National Literacy Strategy: Framework for Teaching, HMSO

Godwin, D. and Perkins, M. (1998) Teaching Language and Literacy in the Early Years, David Fulton

Wray, D. and Medwell, J. (1991) Literacy and Language in the Primary Years, Routledge

Lewis, M. and Wray, D. (1995) Developing Children's Non Fiction Writing: Working with Writing Frames, Scholastic

Lewis, M. and Wray, D. (1997) Extending Literacy: Children Reading and Writing Non-fiction, Routledge

Mallett, M. (1999) Informational Reading and Writing in the Early and Primary Years, Routledge

Neate, B. (1995) Finding out about Finding Out: A Practical Guide to Children's Information Books, Hodder and Stoughton

Norman, K. (ed) (1992) Thinking Voices, Hodder & Stoughton

SCAA (1997) Use of Language: A Common Approach, SCAA

Smith, B. (1994) Through Writing to Reading, Routledge

Wing Jan, L. (1991) Write Ways - Modelling Writing Forms, Oxford University Press

Wragg, E. C. et al (1998) Improving Literacy in the Primary School, Routledge

Publications supporting language in design and technology

Ager, R. (1998) Curriculum Bank: Design and Technology Key Stage 2, Scholastic (P)

Bennington, K. (1996) National Curriculum Blueprints: Design and Technology Key Stage 1, Stanley Thorne (P)

Bennington, K. (1996) National Curriculum Blueprints: Design and Technology Key Stage 2, Stanley Thorne (P)

Benson, C. (1998) Curriculum Bank: Design and Technology Key Stage 1, Scholastic (P)

DATA (1995) Technical Vocabulary for Key Stages 1 and 2, DATA

DATA (1996) Primary Co-ordinators' File, DATA

DATA (1995) Primary Guidance Materials for Key Stages 1 and 2, DATA

DATA (1999) DATA Helpsheets, DATA

Design Council (1991) Stories as Starting Points for Design and Technology (video resource pack), Design Council

DfE (1995) Design and technology in the National Curriculum, DfE

Educational Communications (1997) Make It, Bake It* (P)

Educational Communications (1999) The Food File* (P)

Johnson, Paul (1990) A Book of One's Own: Developing Literacy through Making Books, Hodder & Stoughton

Johnson, Paul (1999) Making Books, A&C Black

QCA (1999) A Scheme of Work for Key Stages 1 and 2: Design and Technology, QCA

Ritchie, R. (1995) Primary Design and Technology - A Process for Learning, David Fulton

SCAA (1997) Design and Technology and the use of Language, SCAA

Sweet, Babs (1997) 'I Think DT should stand for Deep Thinking - Design and Technology - The Early Years', in Whitebread, D. (ed) Teaching and Learning in the Early Years, Routledge

There are many LEAs and SATROs who have produced their own material to help teachers with planning appropriate links. Check with individual authorities.

(P) denotes 'includes photocopiable sheets for pupil use'

*Make It, Bake It (KS2) and The Food File (KS1 and 2) are available to schools free of charge, tel: 0171 453 4684

Publications aimed at children

Many story books or poems can be used as a starting point for a design and make activity. Skim the book to look for a need or purpose for something that the children can make. For example, a container in which to hide or carry something; clothes for a character in the story; puppets which the children can use to enact the storyline; food for a journey, party or picnic; or a vehicle to help someone escape, to go on a visit or to replace a broken one.

The following books can be used both for information and/or for a starting point for a design and make assignment. They are organised by design and technology focus.

Key Stage 1

Food

This is the Bear and the Picnic Lunch, Scholastic

Honey Biscuits, Scholastic

Food for Festivals, Longman

Round the World Cookbook, Longman

You can Make Your own Book, Longman

Do People Eat Flowers?, Collins Educational

Pineapple Pizza, Collins Educational

Food, A&C Black Messages series

Mechanisms

Wheels and Axles, Scholastic

Let's Look Inside the Red Car, Scholastic

Let's Look Inside the Yellow Truck, Scholastic

Emergency Rescue, Scholastic

Traffic, Collins Educational

Moving Joints, Scholastic

Which Way, Ben Bunny?, Scholastic

Lighthouse Keeper's Lunch, Longman

Mrs Armitage on Wheels, Collins Picture Lions

Transport, A&C Black Messages series

Structures

I Like this Park, Collins Educational

Buildings, A&C Black Messages series

Textiles

Clothes, A&C Black Messages series

For IDEAS and FPTs

What is Missing?, Collins Educational

Houses, Collins Educational

Cut and Join, Collins Educational

How would you Mend it?, Collins Educational

What's Inside? Toys, Dorling Kindersley

The Way Things Work, Dorling Kindersley - book and CD-ROM

Key Stage 2

Control: mechanisms

Simple Machines, Usborne

The Trap, Collins Educational

developing language through design and technology

The Kingfisher Book of How Things Work, Kingfisher Books

Control: electrical

Electricity, Toy Box Science Series, A&C Black

Food

Starting Cooking, Usborne

What's Cooking, Collins Pathways

Bread, A&C Black Threads series

Finding Out About Food: A Food Dictionary*

Materials

Clay, A&C Black Threads series

Paper, A&C Black Threads series

Bricks, A&C Black Threads series

Wood, A&C Black Threads series

Structures

Starting Design and Technology - Structures, Roger Bull, Series editor John Cave, Cassell

Bridges go from Here to There - Forrest Wilson, The Preservation Press, Washington, USA

Textiles

Why Jumpers are Woolly, Longman

Why T-shirts are Cotton, Longman

Why Leggings are Lycra, Longman

Why Fabrics can Fly, Longman

Wool, A&C Black Threads series

Batik and Tie-Dye - Arts and Crafts Series, Wayland

Stencils and Screens - Arts and Crafts Series, Wayland

Weaving - Arts and Crafts Series, Wayland

For IDEAS and FPTs

The Visual Dictionary of Everyday Things, Dorling Kindersley

What's Inside? Toys, Dorling Kindersley

*'Finding Out About Food: A Food Dictionary' is available free of charge from the National Dairy Council, tel: 0171 499 7822